Small wonder the churches quiesce, pastors fall into sexual sin, congregations languish, and evangelism is a quaint forgotten concept. When few study Biblical prophecy and pastors have neither the knowledge nor the interest to preach the rich doctrines of the Lord's Return, all of that and much more is the certain consequence. Thank God for Dr. Mark Ballard and Dr. Timothy Christian whose love for Christ gave them the courage to write about the coming Christ and the Rapture of every living believer! Read this volume, begin proclaiming the whole counsel of God and the revival we all long for will doubtless come. But a truncated gospel that is agnostic about the end-times is notoriously anemic and provides assurance to few.

Were I to be able to alter one thing about the future, I would have every preacher and prospective theologian under thirty years of age read this book, *Does the Rapture Still Matter?* Set your pulpit and your classroom ablaze with the doctrine of Christ's return and the church will experience the latter rains. Climb out of the morass of negativism that grips the church today! This same Jesus will come again as you have seen Him go.

Paige Patterson
Sandy Creek Foundation

If you are a typical Southern Baptist you have probably not heard many sermons on End times, the Rapture, or the Second Coming of Christ in the last two or three decades. Mark Ballard and Tim Christian have pulled together a very useful overview of biblical teachings on the End Times, the Rapture, and the

Second Coming of Christ. Many will find their identification of key Scripture passages and concise explanations of various points of views on these issues to be very helpful. Get ready to find yourself drawn to God's Word to see afresh what God says about what lies ahead.

Chuck Kelley
President Emeritus,
Distinguished Research Professor of Evangelism,
New Orleans Baptist Theological Seminary

My first encounter with teaching on the Rapture was in seminary. The textbooks were written by Dwight Pentecost and John Walvoord. Later, there was a move from the scholarly approach to the popular approach by Tim Lahaye, Hal Lindsey, and others. Mark Ballard and Tim Christian, in their work *Does the Rapture Still Matter?*, bridge the scholarly and the popular. The authors are to be commended for writing a work that is well researched yet easy to read. Also, given the dearth of serious works on the topic of the Rapture in the last 25 years, I appreciate the authors' effort to bring to our attention afresh why the Rapture still matters.

James Flanagan
President Emeritus,
Luther Rice College and Seminary

One day the Lord will return for his saints, both those living and those awaiting the resurrection who have died. He will come as we will be "snatched-up" and meet Him in the air to be with Him for eternity. Mark Ballard and Tim Christian have given us a clear statement of the things that must happen till that day dawns, and what will happen after we experience the rapture of the saints. These pages are a clear presentation of the biblical revelation and the blessed hope that resides in the hearts of believers. These pages will cause each reader to carefully examine their own faith and relationship with the Lord Jesus Christ. We may differ about all the details of that event, but we need to be reminded that this event is not from man's imagination, but from the clear Word of God Who reveals the reality of the rapture as the clear promise from God and the glorious entrance of all believers into the eternal Kingdom of our God! Read with confidence and your faith will be grounded in God's Word and your spirit will be energized by the truth that Our Lord is soon coming to take us to be with Him!

Jimmy Draper
President Emeritus,
LifeWay

From time to time, it is necessary for good basic publications to revisit the rapture question. The title asks a question (does the rapture still matter?) and correctly answers it with a resounding "yes!" The book gives an uncomplicated presentation of the issue of the rapture including its pre-tribulational timing. Ballard and Christian also show an irenic spirit as they deal with controversial views. While readers may disagree with fine points, this work is an important survey in a day when eschatology is erroneously considered passé and not helpful for Christian living today. A believer can actually grow and be enriched in the reading. I heartily endorse this work to the Christian public.

Mike Stallard
Vice President for International Ministries,
Friends of Israel Gospel Ministries

In their book *Does the Rapture Still Matter?*, Mark Ballard and Tim Christian cleverly and convincingly define, discusse, and defend the importance of the rapture as a distinctive theological foundation of a biblical church. Nowadays in which suspicion about the end times and a sense of science fiction speculation is growing, the reader will find in this book certainty of his faith for the present and for the future. Our faith is unshakable: Jesus is coming for His Bride.

Javier Chavez
Senior Pastor,
Iglesia Bautista Amistad Cristiana International

It is hard to imagine a more concise, substantive, biblical, and thought-provoking book explaining the Rapture than *Does The Rapture Still Matter?* The authors graciously and efficiently dispel a host of errors about the rapture and second coming. Mark and Timothy do this while weaving a tapestry of the gospel, the bodily resurrection of Christ and his followers, and the blessed hope (Titus 2:12-13) that inspires Christians with spir-

itual confidence by which to live; it is both richly theological and inspirational for the layman and pastor alike.

Ronnie W. Rogers
Senior Pastor
Trinity Baptist Church, Norman, OK

Nothing excites believers like the hope found in
Bible prophecy. Yet, too many refuse to study it because
books are confusing and hard to understand. Mark Ballard and Tim Christian, however, have written this easy
to understand book that will refresh your spirit, encourage your heart, and have you listening for a shout!

Phil Waldrep
Phil Waldrep Ministries

Yes, I believe the Rapture still matters! I am so
thankful to Mark and Tim for addressing this compelling biblical subject. This book is highly informative,
deeply inspirational, and very encouraging. While the
subject of the Rapture comforts all who follow Christ, it
also calls us to finish the task of taking the Good News
of Jesus Christ to every person in the world. This is
why the Rapture stills matters!

Ronnie W. Floyd
Pastor Emeritus,
Cross Church
Past President of the Southern Baptist Convention
and the National Day of Prayer

To those who claim that rapture theology is irrelevant to Christian discipleship, Mark Ballard and Tim Christian answer "Teaching and preaching about the Rapture is not a hindrance to or a distraction from growing in grace. I am convinced the opposite is true." This highly accessible treatise makes it clear that what we believe about the future has indelible effects on how we behave in the present. And no doctrine in all of Christian theology gives more motivation to live for Christ in the here-and-now than the imminent or "pre-tribulational" rapture of the church. Written from the heart of two pastors who believe the Bible is inerrant and should be understood in its grammatical and historical contexts, *Does the Rapture Still Matter?* is perfect for those in the church who need be reminded of the urgency of the coming "blessed hope"—and why that should spur them on to be a loving neighbor and proclaiming the gospel while there's still time.

Cory M. Marsh
Professor of New Testament,
Southern California Seminary
Co-editor of Discovering Dispensationalism:
Tracing the Development of Dispensational Thought
from the First to the Twenty-First Century

Mark Ballard and Tim Christian have brought the evangelical church face to face with a long neglected and currently denied doctrine of the Rapture. Unfortunately, in most evangelical churches the leadership takes the position that the "rapture does not matter." The authors describe this attitude as "Rapture-Indifference."

With theological skill and exegetical acumen, the authors traverse I Thessalonians 4:13-18, I Corinthians 15:50-58, and John 14 in chapters 3-5. In my opinion, these chapters constitute the strength of the book. The arguments are not new, but they are reminders of a doctrine that has been shelved far too long.

One other strength is noteworthy, the authors review the various rapture positions with clarity and fairness to the respective traditions. Their presentation reveals the scholarship we have come to expect from Mark Ballard and Tim Christian. This book is worthy of your time. It will serve the pastor in the pulpit, the professor in the classroom, the student who seeks to understand the issues, and of course the church member in the pew will be enriched by it's positive content in the Hope of a better day!

Marvin Jones, PhD
President,
Montana Christian College

A quick survey of the nightly news and the daily times will remove any doubt—the world is indeed heading with growing rapidity toward chaos and turmoil. Wars and rumors of war, pain and destruction, the breakdown of the family, and subjective versions of truth are all on full display as society and culture continually darken. The doctrines of the end times are perhaps the most pertinent, yet all too often neglected, topics in all of Christendom. Few leaders have the fortitude to address such topics with alacrity and confidence. I am grateful that Mark Ballard and Tim Christian have delved into the depths where few others are willing to navigate. *Does the Rapture Still Matter?* properly focuses on what the Scripture says regarding the rapture and the role of Christians in the end times. Pastors, scholars, Bible teachers, and church members alike will do well to pick up this brief volume and likely will find they have trouble putting it down.

Z. Scott Colter, PhD
Assistant Professor,
Mid-America Theological Seminary
Executive Director,
Conservative Baptist Network
Partner,
Colter & Co.

This is one of those resources that will both inform you about End-Time events and set your heart ablaze with anticipation of seeing Jesus as He returns for His church. Additionally, it will give you a deep sense of urgency to share the Gospel with our cities, nation and world while there is still time. Let's be about our Father's work before He comes!

Brad Jurkovich,
Senior Pastor,
First Baptist Church, Bossier City, LA
Spokesman,
Conservative Baptist Network

Does the
RAPTURE
Still Matter?

Does the
RAPTURE
Still Matter?

Mark H. Ballard
and
Timothy K. Christian

NORTHEASTERN BAPTIST PRESS

Bennington, Vermont

CONTENTS

FOREWORD

by

Stephen Rummage

Not many years ago, I sat next to a friend and fellow professor at a chapel service in one of our Southern Baptist seminaries. The chapel congregation was singing the old gospel hymn written by Fanny Crosby, "Jesus, Keep Me Near the Cross." With the newest edition of the *Baptist Hymnal* in our hands, we sang the words of the refrain:

> *In the cross, in the cross*
> *Be my glory ever,*
> *Till my ransomed soul shall find*
> *Rest beyond the river.*

I noticed that my friend stopped singing during the next stanza. He was looking closely at the lyrics, and he nudged me and whispered, "They changed the words of this song." I asked, "Really?" He answered, "Yes, in the older hymnals, the lyrics were 'raptured soul,' not 'ransomed soul.'"

Sure enough, a quick investigation revealed that earlier versions of the *Baptist Hymnal*, and, interestingly, even the more recent editions of Lutheran and Methodist hymnals, render the lyrics of the chorus as Fanny Crosby originally wrote them:

> *In the cross, in the cross*
> *Be my glory ever,*
> *Till my raptured soul shall find*
> *Rest beyond the river.*

I wouldn't pretend to know what rationale some Baptist hymnal editorial committee might have had in changing Fanny Crosby's lyrics. The altered version is certainly theologically accurate and orthodox. When our souls find eternal rest, it will indeed be because they have been ransomed by the blood of Jesus.

Still, here's what bothers me: Fanny Crosby didn't write "ransomed soul," and no one really had any business changing what she wrote! Her vivid imagery of a fountain of healing streams, heaven with its golden streets, and eternal rest beyond the river of death, included the assurance that her soul would be raptured. To change the text was to abridge her faith.

The volume that you hold in your hands is a strong and unabridged expression of faith, based on compelling biblical evidence, that the souls of believers who are "alive and remain" at the return of Christ for His church will be "caught up" to meet the Lord in the air (1 Thessalonians 4:17) — the biblical doctrine commonly known as "the Rapture."

Admittedly, the doctrine of the Rapture often does not receive the serious attention it deserves. Though many, many evangelical, Bible-believing Christians affirm the Rapture, the doctrine has been trivialized in its popular expressions. Consider just a few ways the Rapture pops up in culture:

> » T-shirt slogans (Do a quick internet search for "Rapture Ready," and you'll find several designs).
> » Bumper stickers ("In case of Rapture, this vehicle will be unmanned").
> » Dystopian Christian fiction (See *Left Behind* and its incredibly successful companion products).
> » Dystopian non-Christian fiction (See *The Leftovers* and its not-quite-as successful companion products).

Perhaps because of the trivial and sensationalized way the Rapture has been treated, an increasing number of conservative Christian believers are either down-playing or departing from the doctrine. Much like the embarrassment of the aforementioned hymnal editors at the term, they are editing "rapture" from their vocabularies. Reasons given may include objections that the Rapture is a recently developed doctrine, not found in historic orthodoxy; that Scripture does not actually offer support for believing in the Rapture; or that believing in the Rapture creates an "escape hatch" mentality among Christians that squelches a desire to care about discipleship, suffering, justice issues, the environment, or other pressing needs of humanity.

Within this theological and cultural context, Mark Ballard and Timothy Christian ask the compelling question: *Does the Rapture Still Matter?* They answer with a resounding, "Yes!" With precision and clarity, the authors define the meaning of the Rapture and answers the objections of those who deny it, presents expositions of the major New Testament texts that address the doctrine, examine the different views of the timing of the Rapture, and show the connection between believing in the Rapture and living faithfully for Christ day by day.

For those who share the authors' eschatology (and I find myself in broad agreement with their pretribulational and premillennial perspective), this book offers a helpful approach for understanding the Rapture and teaching the doctrine to others. For those in disagreement, you will find a thoughtful and fair-handed presentation of the Rapture that will provide strong grounds for giving this perspective respectful consideration. For any believer, The authors' work will challenge you to dig into what the Scripture says about the return of Christ.

Does the Rapture matter? Of course it does! I'm thankful for Mark Ballard and Timothy Christian's careful treatment of this subject, and I encourage you to read what they have written carefully, prayerfully, and expectantly, with a Bible in your hand.

Stephen Rummage, Ph.D.
Senior Pastor,
Quail Springs Baptist Church, Oklahoma City

1

Introduction

Advertise a series of sermons on the Rapture or the book of Revelation, and even a small church is almost guaranteed to gain a few attendees. People are interested.

That has been my repeated experience. And by the way, the interest was not limited to a particular region of the country or a particular period of time. I have found it true *wherever* I preached, west or east, south or north, in nearly half of the 50 states. Further, the interest has continued *whenever* I preached over the 40+ years since I began as a 12-year-old 'preacher-boy' in southern Colorado.

Human nature hungers for End Time insights. People wonder, "Could our present-day problems be pointing to prophecies that will soon be fulfilled?" The chaos in our country appears to be on a collision course with catastrophe. "But … could there be a purpose, a silver lining, in it all? Is the end near? Has Jesus just now risen from His throne to walk toward heaven's exit gate? Is He about to step down into the clouds to Rapture the saints?"

Nearly every time I announce an eschatological topic, guests, including some curious unbelievers, come for the series. Even they want to know what a Bible preacher has to say about the end of the world.

My experience and the experiences of like-minded pastors indicate that people in the pews and some in the general populace remain curious about the Rapture. Yet, that may not be the case among the clergy in general.

Serving as a Baptist College President and a Publisher opens opportunities for regular conversations with 'conservative' pastors, professors, and authors. They are ready to discuss various biblical and theological issues. Yet, many of these resist discussing the End Times. In fact, they are particularly allergic to discussing the Rapture. When I bring up the subject, which I am not hesitant to do, some common responses are:

> » "I'm a pan-millennialist. I believe it'll all pan-out in the end."
> » "I really haven't studied eschatology enough to have an opinion about it."

» "Too controversial. I try to avoid the topic."
» "All I know is that one day Jesus is coming back."
» "I don't have time to think about that kind of stuff. I'm focused on helping people live a faithful Christian life now. Speculating about the End Times doesn't wind my clock."
» "God didn't call me to debate. He called me to make disciples."

SERMON SURVEY

Recently I assigned my summer intern, Tyler Ballard (not a relative), to survey the sermons of twelve specific evangelical preachers. Each of these men shepherds a large church. From their strategic pulpits, their messages are broadcast via radio, television, and podcasts. I asked Tyler to research how many sermons about the Rapture each of the twelve had preached in the past three years. In light of the interest in the pews and the populace, the results were somewhat surprising. In the previous three years:

» 3 out of 12 preached two sermons on the Rapture.
» 1 out of 12 preached five sermons on the topic—4 were part of a series; the 5th was on a separate occasion.
» 8 out of 12 had no available sermons on the Rapture or the End Times.

The research, while limited and anecdotal, may be revealing. Out of a combined total of more than 1800 sermons [at least 150 sermons from each of the twelve popular, influential conservatives], only eleven sermons proclaimed the Rapture. Does this research indicate two-thirds of these 'Bible-teachers' do not think the Rapture is an urgent topic? To be transparent, I suspect that to be true. Why else would one fail to address the topic within a three-year period? We don't ignore things we believe are urgent.

Further, does ignoring the Rapture and the End Times Scriptures indicate a trend in the evangelical community? If so, is it a good trend or a bad one? Are the so-called 'End Times Scriptures' so sparse and their interpretations so speculative that ignoring the topic actually reveals faithfulness to the Bible?

You be the judge. "Bible prophecy makes up one-fourth of the written Word of God."[1] Further, "from Genesis to Revelation," there are no less than "one thousand predictive prophecies. Half of these have already been literally fulfilled, indicating that the other half will yet be literally fulfilled as well."[2] Do you believe intentionally ignoring five hundred unfulfilled Bible prophecies, some of which cover multiple Bible chapters, is a mark of faithfulness to the Bible?

The closer we get to the Rapture, the more an indifference toward the topic is growing—at least among pastors and professors. When asked, "Does the Rapture Still Matter?" it appears a majority answer, "No. It doesn't matter; it's not a priority in my preaching and teaching."

If my anecdotal evidence proves accurate and the clergy have largely embraced either "Rapture-agnosticism" or "Rapture-indifference," should we be surprised if confusion and doubt reigns among church members? I think not. What else would we expect?

Hindson and Hitchcock observed, "More and more believers today appear to be agnostic about issues related to the end times, especially the timing of the Rapture."[3] Further, a 2016 LifeWay Research survey of End Time beliefs revealed 25% of those surveyed did not believe the Rapture would be a literal event.[4]

Even so, hunger for End Times truth continues. I have seen it among our college students and among local church members in the northeast.

During the 2021 spring academic semester, Northeastern Baptist College (NEBC) in Bennington, Vermont, offered an intensive study of the Book of Revelation. The course was open to all students in all majors. It was also announced at a handful of local churches. To my surprise, the course had one of the largest enrollments of any course in NEBC history.

Our students have busy schedules. Yet, several took the course as an elective. Likewise, busy local church members participated in the course, even though it met for 3 hours, one evening per week for 15 weeks. All were hungry for a better understanding of the End Times.

To this point, we have described anecdotal evidence of the contrasting attitudes among pastors and professors and people in the pews. However, popular opinion does not determine whether or not the Rapture still matters. Truth is not discovered through opinion polls and surveys. A comfortable majority may be 100% wrong.

The real question is *not*, "How do you feel about the Rapture?" or even, "Are you interested in the Rapture?" The real question is, "What does the Bible teach?" I will attempt to answer this question in the pages of this book.

To begin answering the real question, we will consider what the Bible says about:

1. The nature of the Rapture
2. The timing of the Rapture

Part One (Chapters 2-6) will address the Nature of the Rapture. The Timing of the Rapture will be considered in Part Two (Chapters 7-9). Whenever the Rapture happens, trust me, you do not want to miss it! You can find out how to be certain that you will enjoy the benefits of this great event by reading the Appendix.

Part 1
THE NATURE OF THE RAPTURE

2

Defining and Denying the Rapture

Consider four aspects of the nature of the Rapture. First, we will define the Rapture. Second, we will respond to some who deny the Rapture. Third, we will defend the biblical nature of the Rapture. Fourth, we will distinguish the *Rapture* from Jesus Christ's *Second Coming* to earth.

DEFINITIONS

We begin with a definition. Notice both the technical meaning of the word *Rapture*, and the typical way it is used in eschatological[5] discussions. According to Hindson and Hitchcock, our English word, "*Rapture* comes from the Latin word *raptus*," which is defined,

11

"to snatch up, to seize, or to carry off by force."[6] Theologians and commentators typically use this technical definition in theological discussions.

Theologian Charles C. Ryrie, for example, defined the Rapture as, "The catching away of the church from the earth to heaven."[7] Kimball defines the Rapture as a term "applied to the scriptural event characterizing the translation of the living saints and the resurrection of the dead saints to meet Christ in the air when He returns."[8] Paige Patterson states, "The Latin word Rapture refers to the taking away of every true believer at the time of the *parousia* [Greek] or the coming of Christ."[9] These authors consistently apply the definition, "caught up," when discussing the time when Jesus Christ will return in the clouds to transport the believing church away from earth to heaven.

In his work, *Could The Rapture Happen Today?*, Mark Hitchcock argues that the Bible speaks of *seven different Raptures*. He says six have passed and one remains. Further, Hitchcock argues that *five* of the Raptures are *physical* and *two* are *spiritual*. He refers to Enoch (Gen 5:24; Heb 11:5), Elijah (2 Kgs 2:11), and Jesus (Mark 16:19; Luke 24:51; Acts 1:2) being caught up to heaven as past physical Rapture events.[10] Hitchcock also identifies Philip's miraculous "catching up" and removal to a different location (Acts 8:39-40) as a physical Rapture.[11] He further refers to Isaiah seeing the throne room of heaven (Isa 6:1-8) and Paul seeing the third heaven (2 Cor 12:2-4) as spiritual Raptures.[12] Finally, Hitchcock notes there will be one more physical Rapture: the Rapture of the church.[13]

This brief review includes both the technical meaning and the typical use of the term Rapture in biblical and theological discussions. To the list, I add my own definition below.

MARK BALLARD'S DEFINITION

I too focus on the definition, *caught up*, and demonstrate the connection with the Greek word, *harpadzo*, and the Latin word, *raptus*. The apostle Paul used the Greek word, *harpadzo*, in 1 Thessalonians 4:17. I agree that the best English translation is, *caught up*. The verse states, "Then we who are alive and remain shall be caught up together with them in the clouds to meet the Lord in the air. And thus we shall always be with the Lord." Imagine! The work of formulating a definition should not distract us from the exciting reality of the Rapture.

Based on the technical definition and typical use of the word, I define the *Rapture* as: *the prophesied event that will occur toward the end of the age, when Jesus Christ will return in the clouds with a shout and a trumpet sound, to resurrect the dead believers, transform the living believers, and catch up His true church to meet Him in the air and return with Him to the Father's house in heaven.*

The "true" church includes all who have been saved by grace through faith in Jesus Christ (Eph 2:8-9; John 1:12). I emphasize the "true" church rather than the "visible" church. A visible local church is often a mixture of true and false believers. Their names are on a church membership role, but some of their names are not in the "Lamb's Book of Life" (Rev 21:27). These do not have a genuine saving relationship with Jesus Christ; they are not members of the true church. They profess the right words but do not know Jesus. They have been baptized and may have an impressive record of pious religious service, yet Jesus does not know them (Matt 7:21-23). These religious unbelievers will be left behind at the Rapture. Not a single genuine believer, however, will be left. At the Rapture, all believers, dead and alive, will be *caught up* together to meet Jesus Christ in the air.

Most conservative scholars agree with the definition and usage stated above. Even so, a few conservatives reject the definition. Some even declare, "I do not believe there will be a future *Rapture*."

Denying the Rapture

In 2008, for example, Cecil Maranville stated, "The Rapture, often called 'The Blessed Hope,' is sadly more hoax than hope."[14] Like other Rapture deniers, as well as many who reject the pre-tribulation Rapture, Maranville argues that until John Nelson Darby invented the teaching in the 19th century, no one believed the now-dominate doctrine.[15] Francis X. Gumerlock notes that several theologians have made a similar statement. However, in his 2019 *Biblio Sacra* article, Gumerlock points to evidence that the Rapture was taught long before Darby was born. In fact, his article notes discussions of the Rapture in the 11th century.[16]

Others argue that one should reject the concept because the word *Rapture* is not in the New Testament. Most scholars, however, reject that argument on two grounds. First, a theological word can faithfully represent the Bible's true teaching without the word being in the Biblical text. For example, terms such as Trinity, inerrancy, and hypostatic union are not found in the New Testament text, but without question, the Bible declares the concepts. Second, the word *Rapture* comes from the Latin word, *raptus*.[17] The word Rapture is not in our English New Testament, but it is in the Latin text of 1 Thessalonians 4:17. Again, the Greek word, *harpadzo*, is translated into English, *caught up*, and into Latin as *raptus*.

One of the most aggressive opponents of the pre-tribulation Rapture, Dave MacPherson, wrote two books attacking the position. The titles of his two works demonstrate his contempt for the pre-tribulation view. In 1975 he published, *The Incredible Cover-up: The True Story of the Pre-Trib Rapture*. He continued his attack with, *The Great Rapture Hoax*, in 1983. Despite his contempt for the *pre-tribulation Rapture* position, even MacPherson acknowledged the existence of the *Rapture* as a literal event. In his first book's preface he wrote, "All Bible-exalting persons believe in the 'catching up' of 1 Thessalonians 4, but there is still disagreement on the timing of this event—chiefly whether it happens before the Tribulation or after."[18] Indeed, most evangelical scholars today acknowledge the reality of the *Rapture*, though many differ on the timing of the event.

One reason I am still a Baptist is our longstanding belief that the Bible is the final authority for the faith and practice of the church. Various historical discussions of the *Rapture* can be instructive and helpful. However, in the end, the Scriptures must determine our beliefs about the *Rapture* or any other subject.

The most crucial question is, "Does the Bible teach that believers can and should anticipate an actual future *Rapture*?" We now turn our attention to answering this question.

Defending the Rapture

"Don't let anyone lead you astray," says Mark Hitchcock. "The Rapture is in the Bible. But don't just take my word for it. See it for yourself in the pages of the Word of God."[19] Further, he notes that many passages speak of the *Rapture*, but three texts are crucial.[20] I go a step further. Several Bible passages mention the *Rapture* in passing, but only two describe the *Rapture* in detail; one additional text is a clear reference to the *Rapture* with limited details.

The two descriptive *Rapture* passages (1 Thess 4:13-18; 1 Cor 15:50-58) complement one another. The Apostle Paul describes how believers will be physically transformed. He connects the believers' physical transformation at the *Rapture* with Jesus Christ's physical transformation when He got up from His burial slab and walked out of the tomb in His glorified resurrection body.

In addition, we find the third passage in John's Gospel. John allows us to be flies on the wall, listening in to a special Passover celebration on the night of Jesus's betrayal. Jesus and His disciples were in an upper room. The conversation is often called the Upper Room Discourse. Considering the author's intended meaning in the grammatical-historical context, I see a clear reference to the *Rapture* of Christ's church (John 14:1-6). In the next three chapters we will consider each of these individual passages.

3

Defending the Rapture
Part 1

Do Not Be Ignorant, Brethren
1 Thessalonians 4:13-18

"**B**ut I do not want you to be ignorant, brethren, concerning those who have fallen asleep, lest you sorrow as others who have no hope" (v. 13). Someone once quipped that the 'ignorant brethren' is the largest denomination in the world. We might also add that the statement shows the importance of commas, but that is a different discussion. For Paul, ignorant believers were no laughing matter. He noted his concern at least five times.

The apostle Paul did not want believers to be ignorant about Israel's partial blindness (Rom 11:25), the reason every believer receives at least one spiritual gift (1 Cor 12:1), or the suffering he endured to preach the gospel among the gentiles (2 Cor 1:8). Neither did he want believers to be ignorant of Satan's devices (2 Cor

2:11). Finally, Paul did not want Christians to be ignorant of the deceased believers' glorious future (1 Thess 4:13). And that brings us to our text.

A MISSIONARY TEAM

Paul's second missionary journey (Acts 15:36-18:22) took him into new territories where he won converts, planted churches, and discipled some who became his valued, life-long ministry partners. Barnabas had been Paul's partner on his first missionary journey. Silas replaced Barnabas on the second. In Lystra, Paul met Timothy, a gifted young disciple. As Paul mentored him, he recognized Timothy's call and ministry potential. He saw in Timothy the mind of a scholar, the heart of a shepherd, and the perseverance of a soldier. In turn, Timothy recognized Paul's apostolic authority and leadership. Paul became his spiritual father (1 Tim 1:2). Timothy became "Paul's most cherished pupil, and protégé (1 Cor 4:17; Phil 2:19-22)."[21] When Paul invited him to join the missionary team, Timothy jumped at the opportunity. Moving on from the region around Lystra, they traveled to Troas where Luke joined the team. There in Troas, Paul received the famous Macedonian call that took his team, first to Philippi and then to Thessalonica.

In Thessalonica

The team's ministry in Thessalonica began at the Sabbath service in the local synagogue. There, Paul expounded the Scriptures for three Sabbaths. He explained and demonstrated the clear Old Testament evidence that "Jesus … is the Christ" (Acts 17:3). The response within the congregation shook the synagogue leaders. Some of the Jewish synagogue members "were persuaded" along with "a great multitude of the devout [proselyte] Greeks, and not a few of the leading women" (v. 4). Paul and these new converts established the church at Thessalonica, "but the Jews who were not persuaded, becoming envious, took some of the evil men from the marketplace, and gathering a mob, set all the city in an uproar" (v. 5).

As a result, Paul's ministry among them was brief. He wanted to spend an extended time teaching the new believers, but it wasn't possible. Persecution forced him to leave the city, and we can be thankful.

We Benefit

We benefit greatly by the fact that Paul's ongoing discipleship of the church at Thessalonica was via his pen rather than his pulpit. He wrote two letters to the young church; he clarified and expanded what he taught them during his brief stay. One of the subjects was Jesus Christ's imminent return.

The Thessalonian church therefore anticipated the Rapture. However, as time passed without Christ's return, some believers died. The congregation wondered about the deceased. Did they miss the Rapture? Would they miss out on Christ's earthly kingdom? Were they destined to live as spirits eternally? Or perhaps they didn't go to heaven. Are their bodies and souls sleeping in their tombs, awaiting Christ's return? How would their deaths impact their participation in the Rapture of the church? These and other questions troubled them.

Paul wrote 1 Thessalonians to encourage the new church and answer their questions. Jesus Christ's promised return is mentioned in every chapter of the book.

The final section of chapter 4 addresses the church's confusion about deceased believers. The passage opens with Paul's purpose. "But I do not want you to be ignorant, brethren, concerning those who have fallen asleep, lest you sorrow as others who have no hope" (1 Thess 4:13). He did not chide the believers for their sorrow.

Grief is neither strange nor sinful. It is a natural part of life. No one is exempt. Grief is a common experience for believers and unbelievers. Yet, a believer's grief is different. It is not hopeless. Even in death, believers have "hope," which is not wishful thinking but is "confident assurance."[22]

Notice, a believer's death, but only a believer's death, is compared to "sleep." Here, Paul used the metaphor twice, once in verse 13 and once in verse 14. He used it other places as well. For example, "Behold, I tell you a mystery: We shall not all sleep, but we shall all be changed" (1 Cor 15:51). The promise is that all believers will not die physically, but all who are in Christ, living and dead, will be "changed," transformed, at the Rapture.

In contrast, Jesus described the death of an unbeliever. A certain rich man "died and was buried. And being in torment in Hades, he lifted up his eyes ..." (Luke 16:22-23). His death was not restful but horrible, and so it will be for all the unsaved.

Paul noted his Thessalonian friends' concern for their fellow believers "who have fallen asleep" (1 Thess 4:13). Charles Ryrie noted that this meaningful metaphor contains at least three enlightening and comforting truths. First, when the body sleeps, one is often unaware of activity around him, but he does not cease to exist. Likewise, the dead believers, though no longer in contact with the living, continue to exist. In fact, they have a conscious existence, as Jesus noted in His story of the believing beggar and unbelieving rich man (Luke 16:22-23). In sleep we continue to exist. Second, sleep is temporary. Likewise, for believers, death is temporary. Third, the sleeper will awake. Likewise, the dead in Christ will be resurrected. Ryrie quoted, "Sleep has its waking, death will have its resurrection."[23]

Therefore, Paul encouraged his friends. Your sorrow is real, but it is not like the sorrow of the hopeless heathen. They have "no hope," but you have great hope. Your separation is temporary. Soon they will awake, and you will be reunited. This hope has a solid foundation. Paul said, "For if we believe that Jesus died and rose again [and certainly we do], even so God will bring with Him those who sleep in Jesus" (1 Thess 4:14). "Those who have fallen asleep" (v. 13) "sleep in Jesus" (v. 14).

I love the fact that the passage begins with "hope" (v. 13) and concludes with "comfort" (v. 18). "Comfort" is the Greek word, *parakaléō*. It is a compound word. The first part, *para*, means "beside" and the second, *kaléō*, means "to call." Combined, it conveys the idea of "being called to one's side to help, aid, comfort, and encourage."[24]

"Comfort" is the only command in this passage: "Therefore, comfort one another with these words" (v. 18). It is a choice. It is something we can choose to do. And notice how: "with these words." Isn't that significant? We can actively use words to discourage one another or to encourage one another. The choice Paul wants us to make is clear. When a brother or sister is grieving for a deceased believer, come along beside them and help, aid, comfort, and encourage them with the Rapture promises. In between offering hope to believers and commanding the believers to comfort one another, the Apostle gave two specific reasons for their hope.

JESUS'S PROMISE

Jesus promised to bring the dead believers with Him when He returns. "For if we believe that Jesus died and rose again, even so God will bring with Him those who sleep in Jesus. For this we say to you by the word of the Lord, that we who are alive and remain until the coming of the Lord will by no means precede those who are asleep" (vv. 14-15).

"Don't worry about the deceased believers," Paul said. "They're OK; they're with Jesus. And when He returns, He'll bring them with Him."

Rooted in Resurrection

Notice why Paul was sure this is true. First, Jesus's promise is rooted in His death and resurrection. Paul began, "For if we believe that Jesus died and rose again …" He was confident his friends in Thessalonica believed in Christ's substitutionary death and satisfactory resurrection, because this is the basic truth of the gospel. Everyone who is saved believes it. Jesus Christ's death was in our place; it was a substitutionary, sacrificial death. He who was sinless endured all the punishment for our sins on the cross. He died in our place and was buried.

On the third day, Jesus rose again, and His resurrection was satisfactory. In other words, the Father demonstrated His full satisfaction with the Son's sacrifice when He raised Him from the dead. Christ was "declared to be the Son of God with power according to the Spirit of holiness, by the resurrection from the dead" (Rom 1:4). He was "delivered up because of our offenses, and was raised because of our justification" (Rom 4:25). In God's eyes, His sacrifice was fully sufficient to pay the world's sin debt. It was all that was necessary to save you and me.

Addressing the Thessalonians' sorrow, Paul continues, "… even so God will bring with Him those who sleep in Jesus." Since Jesus died and rose, He will raise those who died trusting in Him. The unbeliever dies under condemnation. The believer dies free from condemnation (Rom 8:1). At death, the believer's body lies down to rest ("sleep") but will be awakened. At the Rapture, Jesus will bring their spirits from heaven, resurrect and glorify their bodies from the earth, and reunite their spirits and bodies in their resurrection bodies. This will all happen in an instant at the Rapture. As we will note in the next chapter, in 1 Corinthians 15 Paul developed at length this noted connection between our gospel redemption, the resurrection, and the Rapture.

Rooted in Revelation

Second, Jesus's promise is rooted in revelation. Paul continued, "For this we say to you by the word of the Lord" (1 Thess 4:15). Revelation is the source of Paul's knowledge. It was not concocted in a vivid imagination. He did not make it up. It is far more than wishful thinking. It is not a placebo, but a promised reality revealed "by the word of the Lord" (v. 15). The Lord Himself promises hope and comfort through the Rapture.

Who Goes First?

Another key to understanding Jesus's Rapture promise is the meaning of the word translated "precede" (v. 15). The Greek word is *phthano*. The verb means, "*come before, precede*."[25] As evangelical interpreters often note,

"Context is king." The very next verse describes the order of events at the Rapture.

The bodies of those who died trusting in Jesus Christ as their Savior will be the first to rise. The physical bodies of the saints will be resurrected from their graves—new, improved, and glorified. Their spirits, which have been alive and well in heaven since the moment they died (2 Cor 5:8), will return with Christ. At the Rapture, their resurrected and glorified bodies will be caught up and reunited with their returning spirits. The believers who remain alive at the coming of the Rapture will immediately have their bodies transformed into a glorified body and will be caught up together with them. All of this will take place in the twinkling of an eye. The church will then be with her Lord forever.

Because of Jesus's Rapture promise, the Thessalonian believers could have hope, despite the death of their fellow believers. You and I have the same promise, the same hope, and also the same comfort.

JESUS'S PLAN

Next, Paul pointed to Jesus's plan as the second reason the Thessalonian believers could have hope despite the death of their loved ones. Many times, I have thought, "Lord, if you would just let me in on Your plan it would be easier for me to trust You." Rarely does the Lord share the details of His plans. Most often He calls us to simply trust Him and walk by faith. We do so by obeying His Word and the promptings of His Spirit. Walking by faith means being faithful whether I understand or not. Yet, on this occasion, the Lord revealed several details about His plan.

> For the Lord Himself will descend from heaven with a shout, with the voice of the archangel, and with the trumpet of God. And the dead in Christ will rise first. Then we who are alive and remain shall be caught up together with them in the clouds to meet the Lord in the air. And thus, we shall always be with the Lord (vv. 16-17).

"The word of the Lord" reveals a striking number of details about the Rapture. The Apostle Paul records those revealed details in these two verses. No less than 8 aspects of the Rapture are packed into 50 Greek words. He tells us:

1. Who will come
2. How He will come
3. To where He will come

He also revealed:

4. Who will rise first
5. What will happen to those who are alive in the Lord
6. The result of this event

In contrast to sending his angels to do the gathering,[26]

7. Jesus Himself will come to gather His people.

Finally, He shows us:

8. His three-fold method to awaken the dead saints and alert the living saints:

    A. Jesus will shout
    B. The archangel will shout
    C. God's trumpet will sound

Jesus will come in the clouds, but His feet will not touch the earth. Believers will meet Him in the air.

In contrast, Revelation 19 describes Jesus returning all the way to earth. No mention of His coming in the clouds. Below we will discuss the significance of this important contrast.

Paul then reveals Jesus's plan to receive His church. First, those who have died trusting Jesus will be raised from the dead, receive their glorified bodies, and join Jesus in the clouds. Then and only then will the living believers be Raptured, *caught up*, to meet the Lord in the air.

As a final revelation of Jesus's plan, Paul notes the result of the *Rapture*. "Thus, we shall always be with the Lord." Here, Paul brings the question of grief to rest. Death is a temporary separation. It does not eternally separate believing loved ones. A grand reunion awaits all who have trusted Jesus. And the best part of the reunion? Not only will we be together, but we will be together with our Lord—forever!

SUMMARY

First Thessalonians 4:13-18 is one of the Bible's clearest and most detailed descriptions of the Rapture. First, we learn *our Lord's purpose in revealing the Rapture*. He gives *hope* and *comfort* to His troubled followers. They, in turn, are enabled to comfort others who are enduring similar troubles.

Paul clarified the uplifting ministry of comfort to his friends in Corinth. By the way, he was ministering in Corinth when he wrote 1 and 2 Thessalonians. He said, "Blessed be the God and Father of our Lord Jesus Christ, the Father of mercies and God of all comfort, who comforts us in all our tribulation, that we may be able to comfort those who are in any trouble, with the comfort with which we ourselves are comforted by God" (2 Cor 1:3-4).

You've likely heard the story of the young boy who awoke from a bad dream, alone and afraid in his dark room. He called out in the night, "Daddy! I'm scared. I'm all alone." His dad answered, "Don't be afraid, son. You aren't alone; Jesus is with you." After a pregnant pause, the boy called back, "I need somebody with skin on them."

And so it is when God uses someone "with skin on them" to bring His comfort to us in our troubles. Being comforted enables us to become His comforters "with skin on" to others who are troubled or grieving. We can give what we have received. Paul reminds us that the Rapture is one of the comfort-giving promises we can receive and share.

Second, we learn *His promise concerning those who "sleep in Jesus."* Their spirits will return with Jesus to be reunited with their resurrected bodies.

Third, through Paul, *our Lord revealed several crucial details of His plan.* At the Rapture, He will resurrect all dead believers and snatch up all the living believers. The purpose, plan, and promise of the Rapture should settle the issue of whether or not it will be a real future event. While 1 Thessalonians 4 is the only passage that uses the word Rapture (in the Latin text), our understanding of the Rapture is by no means limited to this one passage. In the next chapter we will review another major text that spotlights additional exciting details about the Rapture.

4

Defending the Rapture
Part 2

Behold, a Mystery
1 Corinthians 15:50-58

A shocking reality came to light during the Conservative Resurgence of the Southern Baptist Convention (1979-2000). Some professors at all six of the
SBC seminaries either questioned or denied the bodily
resurrection of Jesus Christ. We had long known this
was true at nearly all of the mainline denominational
seminaries. But, speaking as a Southern Baptist, several
among us warned that 'resurrection deniers' had also
breached the SBC fortress. Some of the deniers were
safely entrenched in tenured Professorial Chairs. From
their lofty perch, they were actively infecting our future pastors, missionaries, professors, and denominational leaders with their unbiblical teaching.[27]

I was a seminary student at the time and had no
public forum or influence. Yet, I knew the warnings

were true; "resurrection deniers" were on faculties of SBC seminaries. I knew because I had heard such teaching in a couple of my classes. Corrective actions were required, and via the Conservative Resurgence, were finally taken.

Now a surprising new challenge lies before us. In recent years, some SBC leaders have added elements to the Gospel. They have done so using subtle, spiritual sounding language. The end result, however, will be anything but spiritual. In doing so, they are in danger of redefining the Biblical Gospel, veiling the way of salvation, and bringing themselves under the Apostle Paul's condemnation.[28] I do not believe the biblical definition of the Gospel is either an unclear or peripheral issue.[29] I will add a bit more detail below.

When it comes to the Rapture, the present day story is a bit different. Few evangelicals deny its existence *in theory*. Nearly all acknowledge that the Bible includes at least a few references to the Rapture. Many, however, deny the Rapture *in practice*. They avoid teaching or preaching about eschatology in general and the Rapture specifically.[30]

In contrast, the apostle Paul was neither silent nor subtle. Toward the end of his first letter to the Corinthian church, Paul dedicated the 58 verses of chapter 15 to declaring and defending three crucial doctrines. The chapter is foundational for understanding:

1. The Gospel
2. The Resurrection of Jesus Christ
3. The Rapture of the church

These are not three isolated subjects; they are interrelated.

THE GOSPEL

First, Paul defined and defended the Gospel (1 Cor 15:1-4). The Gospel message has three tightly interwoven elements that declare what Jesus Christ did to save us (v. 3).

1. Christ died for our sins.
2. Christ was buried.
3. Christ rose from the dead.

All was done "according to the Scriptures" (1 Cor 15:3-4). In other words, Paul did not invent the good news. He simply declared that which the Old Testament prophets declared (v. 1).

Centuries before Paul, God's prophets declared that Israel's promised Messiah would suffer an ignominious, yet vicarious, death. The prophets described the suffering and humiliation of a Roman crucifixion in detail, even including some of the very words Jesus Christ spoke from the cross. Along with Christ's sacrificial death, the prophets predicted the ironic circumstances of His burial and resurrection.[31] Without a doubt, the life, death, and resurrection of Jesus Christ proved Him to be the Messiah (the Christ) promised in the Old Testament.

Paul's Gospel proclamation was consistent (vv. 1-2). He did not modify the Gospel from place to place because he did not originate the Gospel. He was merely the Gospel's conduit. Both then and now, the Gospel is the same for all people in all places at all times.

Elsewhere, in the strongest possible words, the Apostle warns against perverting the Gospel of Christ. He said, "But even if we, or an angel from heaven, preach any other gospel to you than what we have preached to you, let him be accursed" (Gal 1:8). And, just in case we weren't paying attention, he adds, "Now I say again, if anyone preaches any other gospel … let him be accursed" (v. 9).

We must not add to or take away from the true Biblical Gospel. A distorted Gospel is a false gospel, not the one and only saving Gospel.

RESURRECTION

Next, Paul defends Jesus Christ's bodily resurrection (1 Cor 15:5-49). He identifies 14 resurrection eyewitnesses, either by name or by title, noting they were a part of a larger group of more than 500 eyewitnesses. Many of the eyewitnesses were alive at the time he wrote the letter, and he invites the Corinthians to cross-examine them (vv. 5-11). By the way, Paul's testimony has added weight since he too was one of the eyewitnesses.

Central Truth

Paul declares in no uncertain terms that Jesus Christ's physical resurrection is central to the Christian faith. Some in Corinth said, "Impossible. Dead people don't rise. Everyone knows that." Paul answered, "If there is no resurrection of the dead, Jesus Christ did not rise. If Christ is not risen, Christianity is a hoax, and anyone who believes it is a miserable, pathetic dupe" (see vv. 12-19).

Spiritualizing the resurrection, as some do, is unacceptable. In our day some claim, "Believing in a physical resurrection is a bridge too far for intelligent, educated people in a scientific age. But that's okay. One can be a faithful Christian without believing in a literal resurrection. Whether or not Jesus actually got up and walked out of the tomb misses the main point. Jesus was alive in the disciples' hearts, and that's all that mattered. Likewise, He can be alive in our hearts today."

How would Paul respond to a spiritualized resurrection? "Absurd! A 'so called' spiritual resurrection would not be something that happened to Jesus. It would be a delusion inside the head of one who claims to believe it." We cannot have it both ways. Either Jesus Christ is dead and Christianity is false, or Jesus Christ is physically alive and Christianity is true.

Certain Truth

Following the negatives, Paul rushes to add the positive. He declares both Jesus Christ's past resurrection and future reign. His future reign is as certain as His past resurrection. Do not doubt it (vv. 20-34).

Paul also presents additional arguments for the veracity of Jesus Christ's bodily resurrection (vv. 35-49). Not only does Paul illustrate how there can be a resurrection, but he also describes the kind of body we will have. And that brings us back to our subject. Paul ties Jesus's past resurrection to the future resurrection and transformation of all believers.

Having reviewed the chapter's content with broad strokes, notice how the three subjects in 1 Corinthians 15 interrelate. And by the way, this is not theoretical; it is personal. If you believe the Gospel, you are saved (vv. 1-4). If you are saved, you will be resurrected (vv. 5-49), and the Rapture is when you will be resurrected (vv. 50-58).

Rapture

The final section of 1 Corinthians 15 describes a specific moment in time when the physical bodies of the dead "in Christ" will be raised, and the living "in Christ" will be transformed.[32] As we compare this passage with what Paul wrote to his friends in Thessalonica, we notice some distinct details about the Rapture. Yet, it is clear the same event is in Paul's mind as he dictates both letters. The two passages compliment one another and clarify our understanding. Consider Paul's words.

[50] Now this I say, brethren, that flesh and blood cannot inherit the kingdom of God; nor does corruption inherit incorruption. [51] Behold, I tell you a mystery: We shall not all sleep, but we shall all be changed—[52] in a moment, in the twinkling of an eye, at the last trumpet. For the trumpet will sound, and the dead will be raised incorruptible, and we shall be changed. [53] For this corruptible must put on incorruption, and this mortal *must* put on immortality. [54] So, when this corruptible has put on incorruption, and this mortal has put on immortality, then shall be brought to pass the saying that is written:

"Death is swallowed up in victory.
[55] *O Death, where is your sting?*
O Hades, where is your victory?"
[56] The sting of death *is* sin, and the strength of sin *is* the law. [57] But thanks *be* to God, who gives us the victory through our Lord Jesus Christ. [58] Therefore, my beloved brethren, be steadfast, immovable, always abounding in the work of the Lord, knowing that your labor is not in vain in the Lord (1 Cor 15:50-58).

Just as Jesus Christ rose from the dead, so He will resurrect all believers at a specific time in the future—the Rapture. Jesus's resurrection was physical, and the believers' resurrection will be physical. Our hope and assurance of a future resurrection are based on the sure, solid, certain foundation of Jesus's past resurrection. Because He rose from the dead, He will never again experience pain or death. His physical body was transformed from a "corruptible [able to age, deteriorate, and die[33]] body" into an "incorruptible [not able to age, deteriorate, and die[34]] body," and that is our future as well. "Like the dead ([1 Cor 15] vv. 42-43), the living will exchange the temporal and imperfect for the eternal and perfect (cf. 13:10). For those who belong to Christ, death's power will be removed."[35] At the Rapture all believers, living and dead, will be transformed. Consider three important truths Paul taught about our future resurrection and transformation.

Resurrection Hope NOT Fully Realized in This Life

When contemporary Christians speak of the hope of the resurrection, they often refer to our hope in this life. They focus on the here and now. "Since Jesus rose from the dead," they say, "He is able and willing to help His followers face life's troubling trials with grace. We have hope because Jesus is alive in us."

Certainly, we celebrate the comfort and hope Christ gives. No question about it. But present comfort and hope is only the beginning of the story, not the whole story. Our resurrection-inspired hope includes this life and its trials, but it also transcends this life and its trials. That is a good thing, since the afterlife is far longer than this life.

The Apostle Paul said, "If in this life only we have hope in Christ, we are of all men the most pitiable" (1 Cor 15:19). Why is that true? If our hope in Christ is only for the here and now, it is a puny and pathetic hope. In fact, if there is no resurrection, living with eternity in mind is a foolish waste of time. Why should anyone discipline himself and deny himself any fleshly desire? If there is no future resurrection, self-indulgence is the only sensible thing. Paul agreed. He said, "If the dead do not rise, *'Let us eat and drink, for tomorrow we die!'*" (v. 32).

The Christian life, a spiritual, transformed, self-denying life of taking up the cross and following Jesus (Mark 8:34), only makes sense if there is a future resurrection. But that's not all.

Resurrection is an absolute necessity. Paul explains, "Now this I say, brethren, that flesh and blood cannot inherit the kingdom of God; nor does corruption inherit incorruption" (v. 50). Considering the prevalent view of the Kingdom of God among today's evangelicals, that is quite a statement. Allow me to explain.

Overemphasis on Kingdom Now

An Amazon search, "The Kingdom of God," reveals links to hundreds of books. Attend an evangelical conference and it is almost certain you will hear repeated mentions of the Kingdom. Conferences and books about a "Kingdom-Focused Church," "Kingdom-Focused Marriage," "Kingdom-Focused Business," etc., abound. The focus is on believers experiencing God's Kingdom now.

Mark H. Ballard

As a result of this "Kingdom talk," many believers think the Kingdom of God is another name for the church. Wayne Grudem cautions, "We should not identify the Kingdom of God and the church, nor should we see the Kingdom of God as entirely future, something distinct from the church age."[36] I say, "Amen," to the first half of Grudem's statement, but hesitate to affirm the second half. Why? Present day sermons and small group studies so emphasize "Kingdom Now," that the biblical concept of a future Kingdom is either pushed aside as insignificant, or is at best, acknowledged only in passing.

Influenced by Grudem and other popular writers, the statement, "The Kingdom is now and not yet,"[37] is repeated as if it were a full, sufficient, and satisfactory explanation of God's Kingdom. Fewer and fewer sermons declare Jesus Christ's future return to establish His Kingdom.

Above, I described my anecdotal research project. We reviewed the past three years of sermons posted on the websites of twelve well-known and influential preachers. All are self-proclaimed Biblical conservatives. The research revealed that only four of the twelve had preached a message on the Rapture or the End Times in the previous three years. Out of the hundreds of sermons available, only eleven sermons focused on the Rapture. This reality is not new to the

2nd decade of the 21st century, but it seems predominate today.

In a 2015 Northeastern Baptist College chapel sermon, Ronnie Floyd noted, "You don't hear many sermons on the Second Coming of Jesus anymore."[38] Writing in 2016, Hitchcock agreed. "More and more believers today appear to be agnostic about issues related to the end times, especially the timing of the Rapture."[39] Indeed, the emphasis on a present Kingdom, Christ now ruling in believers' hearts and over His churches, has eclipsed the former emphasis on Jesus Christ's second coming to establish the Kingdom of God on earth.

Observations, surveys, and trends are interesting and informative. They help us analyze the theological vigor of a particular era in church history, but trends do not determine truth. God's revelation, preserved in the Bible, is our final authority. Therefore, our primary concern is not what preachers are saying, but what God has said.

Under the Holy Spirit's inspiration the Apostle Paul wrote, "Flesh and blood cannot inherit the Kingdom of God" (1 Cor 15:50). As the Lord Jesus reigns in one's life, from time to time the believer enjoys small foretastes of the glory God has in store for His children. Yet, it is obvious we are not now living in the Kingdom of God. War has not ceased, all weapons have not been transformed into farm implements,[40] and we are still flesh and blood. Only resurrection bodies can truly inherit the Kingdom of God.

Resurrection hope is not fully realized in this life. It will be fully realized only when believers receive their resurrected bodies. Paul describes that hope in the next seven verses of the paragraph.

Ressurection Hope, Fully Realized at the Rapture

The Rapture is a "mystery" (1 Cor 15:51). But what kind of mystery? Paige Patterson notes, "Mystery (*musterion*) does not refer in the Scriptures to a mystery in the sense of unraveling a criminal plot but rather to an understanding which has been given by direct revelation of God."[41] The word emphasizes something that was hidden in the past, but now God has unveiled and revealed it. It was unknown to mankind until God made it known.

Paul stated the content of the newly revealed mystery: "We shall not all sleep, but we shall all be changed" (1 Cor 15:51). This is it! "All"—not the faithful now and the faltering later (no partial rapture), but "all"—who are saved by grace through faith in Jesus Christ will be transformed "in a moment, in the twinkling of an eye" (v. 52). At that sudden, millisecond instant, "the last trumpet … will sound." It will be heard around the globe and in every corridor of heaven.

The Rapture will produce immediate, exciting results. The decayed, corrupted, and disintegrated bodies of the dead believers will suddenly and simultaneously "be raised incorruptible." "Ashes to ashes, dust to dust" bodies will suddenly spring to life, new and glorified.

Also, the living believers "will be changed" (v. 52). Suddenly, their bodies will be "incorruptible" and immortal (v. 53). They will be spiritually and physically transformed and glorified, no longer able to sin, deteriorate, or die. Jesus Christ's death on the cross and resurrection from the grave fully conquered the incorrigible enemies—sin, hell, death, and the grave.

At the Rapture, the victory Jesus Christ won "once for all"[42] will instantly become a fully realized reality in all the saints. Even gravity will no longer hold them. As noted above, the unfolding mystery is also described in 1 Thessalonians 4:13-18.

Compare the Passages

Consider how the two passages support and supplement one another. Paul assures his friends in both

Corinth and Thessalonica that Jesus will return (1 Cor 15:23; 1 Thess 4:16) to resurrect the dead believers and transform the living believers (1 Cor 15:52; 1 Thess 4:16). He will do this "in a moment, in the twinkling of an eye, at the last trumpet. For the trumpet will sound, and the dead will be raised incorruptible, and we shall be changed" (1 Cor 15:52). A "shout" and "the voice of an archangel" will accompany "the trumpet of God" (1 Thess 4:16).

The Apostle assures his friends in Thessalonica that when Jesus Christ returns, He will resurrect the dead believers, and translate them along with the living believers. "And the dead in Christ will rise first. Then we who are alive *and* remain shall be caught up together with them in the clouds to meet the Lord in the air. And thus we shall always be with the Lord" (1 Thess 4:16b-17).

To the church at Corinth Paul states that Christ will resurrect the dead believers and transform all believers, living and dead (1 Cor 15:51). In his letter to the Thessalonians, Paul adds that the spirits of those who died in Christ will return with Jesus to be re-united with their now resurrected, glorified bodies (1 Thess 4:16-17). The promised transformation and translation are not contradictory facts. They are complimentary truths.

Purpose of the Passages

Each passage had a specific focus and purpose in its context. Paul stated specific facts about the Rapture to correct a false idea that troubled the Thessalonians, and another idea that confused the Corinthians.

Troubles at Thessalonica

We can summarize the question that troubled the believers in Thessalonica. During Paul's time in the city[43] it seems he taught the new church about Jesus Christ's Deity, death, resurrection,[44] imminent Rapture,[45] and Christ's Second Coming at the end of the tribulation[46] to set up His kingdom on earth. Jesus will be the righteous King, judging the nations and reigning over the world.

Envious opponents among Paul's fellow countrymen twisted his teaching. They used them to accuse the new Christians of treasonous activities. "These are all acting contrary to the decrees of Caesar, saying there is another king—Jesus" (Acts 17:7). Jason, one of the church members, was arrested and heavily fined for harboring insurrectionists, Paul and Silas, in his home. Whether or not the evidence substantiated the charge was beside the point. The missionaries managed to escape only because the brethren hid them until they were able to slip away under cover of darkness.[47]

In spite of persecution, hope remained high among the Thessalonian believers. They anticipated Jesus Christ would return during their lifetimes. However, time passed and a few of the believers died. Their believing family and friends wondered what that meant for the dead. Had they missed out on Christ's coming kingdom?

Whether it was simply a troubling question among believers or a false teaching that took root in the church, we cannot be certain. The text, however, seems to favor the former.

Paul opened the paragraph with comforting rather than confrontational words.[48] He said, "I do not want you to be ignorant, brethren, concerning those who have fallen asleep, lest you sorrow as others who have no hope" (1 Thess 4:13). They were fearful that their "lately deceased [friends] … would be excluded from the glory which [only] those found alive [at Christ's return] … should share."[49]

"Evidently these young Christians felt that those who died before the return of Christ would miss out. They must have thought there was a special advantage to being alive at Christ's return. This meant, in their minds, that there was a disadvantage for those who did not make it."[50]

Paul intended to comfort the distressed.[51] He reassured them that deceased believers are neither forgotten nor excluded; they are included in God's plan. When they died, their bodies remained on earth, but their spirits did not. Their spirits went to be with Jesus in heaven. Those same people will return with Him at the Rapture. At that moment their bodies will be resurrected, glorified, and caught up, and their spirits and glorified bodies will be reunited. New, complete, and totally transformed, they will return to heaven with Jesus.

All believers will be with Jesus for eternity, but those who die before the Rapture are currently with Him in their spirit only and do not yet have their resurrection bodies. I make no claim of understanding it all. It is a part of the mystery of life after death. It is clear, however, that our resurrection bodies will make our experience of eternity in heaven even more glorious than what the deceased believers are experiencing now. Apparently, eternity with our Lord Jesus will become better and better and better as the eons of eternal ages unfold. Resurrection hope is not fully realized in this life, but it will be fully realized at the Rapture. Therefore, the revelation of the Rapture, when rightly understood, comforts believers.

Confusion at Corinth

A different and definitely false teaching confused the church at Corinth. "Some among you," said Paul, "say that there is no resurrection of the dead" (1 Cor 15:12).

Paul confronts the false teaching head on. He declares and defends Jesus Christ's bodily resurrection. He warns that the false doctrine crumbles the very foundation of the Christian faith. "But if there is no resurrection of the dead, then Christ is not risen" (v. 13). When one builds personal faith on a crumbling foundation, it collapses. It can't do anything else. "If Christ is not risen, then our preaching *is* empty and your faith *is* also empty" (v. 14).

Without a literal physical resurrection, our Savior is still dead and buried, our faith is meaningless, and it's as empty as a limp sail on a stranded ship in a windless, glassy sea. And to make matters worse, we are still in bondage to our sins, the dead in Christ are beyond hope, and we are the saddest saps on earth for believing an absurd lie (vs. 17-19). No one is coming to our rescue.

Yet, Paul quickly interjected, "But now Christ is risen from the dead" (v. 20), and that flips all the bad news on its head. He "has become the firstfruits"—the first part of the harvest that assures an even greater harvest is coming—"of those who have fallen asleep" (v. 20). Since Jesus rose, all who receive Him by faith will also rise. "For … in Christ all shall be made alive" (v. 22)—not just spiritually, as great as that is, but physically and eternally as well.

Jesus Christ's resurrection was necessary; it was indispensable. God's entire redemption plan rests on a resurrected, living Savior. Why? Two reasons.

First, our redemption required a blood sacrifice. "And according to the law almost all things are purified with blood, and without shedding of blood there is no remission" (Heb 9:22). To be the redemptive sacrifice for us, Jesus Christ had to die by shedding His blood—and this He did. Therefore, "in Him [Jesus] we have redemption through His blood, the forgiveness of sins, according to the riches of His grace" (Eph 1:7).

Second, our redemption requires a living Redeemer. To hear repentant prayers and save sinners, the Redeemer has to be alive. Again, the salvation plan depends on it. "If you confess with your mouth the Lord Jesus and believe in your heart that God has raised Him from the dead, you will be saved" (Rom 10:9). The dead hear no prayers, but Jesus can hear you. A dead Savior cannot save, but Jesus can save you.

How can the Savior die, yet still be alive to hear and save sinners? That is Paul's point. "But now Christ is risen from the dead" (1 Cor 15:20). The gospel is true because Jesus is alive. He who died also rose from the grave on the third day (vv. 3-4).

Jesus Christ's resurrection was necessary. He is the first fruit, and we are some of His following fruit. Thus, the resurrection and transformation of believers is also necessary. Without it we would be excluded from His Kingdom. "Now this I say, brethren, that flesh and blood cannot inherit the kingdom of God; nor does corruption inherit incorruption" (v. 50). A dying body of "flesh and blood cannot" live in the eternal heavenly glory of God; it is unequipped to do so. Therefore, "this corruptible must put on incorruption, and this mortal *must* put on immortality" (v. 53).

When will the glorious resurrection and transformation happen? At the Rapture (vv. 51-52).

The Last Enemy

Sometimes believers speak of death as if it is our friend. According to the Bible, however, death is our enemy. Paul identified it as "the last enemy" (v. 26). Presently, believers do not have victory over death. We only have victory over the fear of death (Heb 2:15). Unless the Rapture takes place first, everyone reading these words will die. Even so, we have wonderful hope and victory.

Victory

When believers die, just as when unbelievers die, their bodies cease to function and begin to decay. This is the natural process in a fallen world. The believer's body remains on earth, but a believer's spirit is "absent from the body" and instantly "present with the Lord" (2 Cor 5:8). The unbeliever's spirit is absent from the body and instantly separated from the Lord in Hell (Luke 16:23-24).

We previously noted that Paul described the believer's death as "sleep," mentioning it three times in relation to the Rapture (1 Thess 4:13-14; 1 Cor 15:51). It is a metaphor that gives hope and comfort to the loved ones of a deceased believer. Some have robbed it of its beauty, comfort, and encouragement by woodenly interpreting the metaphor. They claim Paul taught that at death a believer's body and soul lie down to sleep unconsciously in the grave until the resurrection, when both body and soul will be awakened, and they will suddenly be aware. The Bible, however, does not teach "soul sleep," the belief that "the dead are not conscious between death and resurrection."[52] These interpreters have made two vital errors: a biblical error and a theological error.

The *biblical error* is obvious when one reads the verses in their context. "Those who have fallen asleep," that is, they died physically, are "asleep in Jesus" (1 Thess 4:13-14). But that does not mean they are unconscious. These very verses that use the metaphor also alert us to the great hope that Jesus will soon return and bring those who sleep in Jesus with Him. In their biblical context, the passages teach that deceased believers are with Jesus and will return with Him when He comes. They haven't missed the resurrection. They will be active participants in the resurrection.

The *theological error* is that 'soul sleep' makes the body and soul a strict unit that cannot be separated, even at death. Therefore, when the body ceases to function, the soul ceases to function. When the body sleeps, the soul sleeps.[53] However, the Bible teaches that both believers and unbelievers are conscious after death. It "is an integral part of the Lord's account of the rich man and Lazarus (Luke 16:19-31). … [Further,] John saw the souls of martyrs in heaven conversing with the Lord after their deaths (Rev 6:9-10)."[54]

Even so, our total victory over death awaits our resurrection bodies that will be like Jesus's resurrected body. Then and only then "shall be brought to pass the saying that is written: *'Death is swallowed up in victory.'*" (1 Cor 15:54)

Our moment of final, ultimate victory over "the last enemy" will happen at the moment the trumpet sounds. In that instant the corrupted bodies of dead believers will rise, "incorruptible"; living believers will be "changed" (1 Cor 15:52). The resurrection and transformation moment, the victory moment, is the moment we call the *Rapture*. Anticipating this total victory gives us hope and comfort (1 Thess 4:13, 18).

Praise

The Rapture also inspires praise. Via illusions to Isaiah 25:8 and Hosea 13:14,[55] Paul exults in our future total victory over "*death*" and "*Hades*" (1 Cor 15:54-55). "Death" is easy enough to understand, but perhaps the word "Hades" gives us a bit more trouble. I have found Charles Hodge's note helpful. He stated:

> The Greek word Hades means, *what is unseen, the invisible world*, the abode of the dead in the widest sense. [The word is used in other passages as well.] It depends on the context whether the immediate reference be to the grave, the place of departed spirits, or hell, in the modern sense of the word. Here where … reference is to the bodies of [the saved] … and to the delivery of them from the power of death, it is properly rendered the grave.[56]

The victory that Isaiah and Hosea prophesied, some 800 years before Paul, will be fulfilled. Whether we are among the living or the dead, when Jesus Christ appears in the clouds, we will experience this glorious victory. Neither death nor the grave will be able to hold our bodies captive. We will be snatched up with all the saints, and that will be glory.

Explanation

Paul's exclamation of praise (vv. 54–55) led into a brief explanatory digression (vv. 56–57). He wants to be sure we understand how truly great our total victory over sin and the grave will be. The digression includes both explanation and thanksgiving.

First, the explanation. Responding to the exclamation's initial question, *"O Death, where is your sting?"* (v. 55), Paul answers, "The sting of death is sin, and the strength of sin is the law" (v. 56).

We are familiar with Paul using vivid metaphors to describe sin's lethal power. For example, sin earns wages; "The wages of sin is death" (Rom 6:23). Since Adam and Eve ate the forbidden fruit in the Garden, death has infected 100% of humanity.[57] "Therefore, just as through one man sin entered the world, and death through sin, and thus death spread to all men, because all sinned" (Rom 5:12). Sin spreads like a fatal virus and no one is immune.

Here, Paul used a different metaphor with an identical outcome—death. "The sting of death is sin" (1 Cor 15:56a). The word translated "sting" describes a painful scorpion sting or the burning pain of a poisonous snakebite.[58] I'm reminded of the "fiery serpents" that tormented and killed many of the rebellious Israelites in the wilderness (Num 21:6). Even though sin gives some "passing pleasures" (Heb 11:25), ultimately it is as painful and as deadly as the lethal venom of Africa's sub-Saharan black mamba.

Paul wants us to ask the urgent question, "Is there an anti-venom for the deadly sting of sin?" Over the years I've heard many answer that question, "Try harder. Do your best to obey God's law." They harbored the vain hope that someday, somehow, they would clean up their acts, try harder, and finally begin obeying the 10 Commandments. They hoped to earn God's favor and get a last-second ticket to heaven.

Several years ago, my wife and I had the privilege of planting a church in New Hampshire. Within the first few months of the work we met a family with whom we connected rather quickly. Both the husband and wife had some church background. However, the husband's background was set in a denomination that failed to proclaim the Gospel message. He was a "good man" who loved his family and desired to please God. However, early on his wife told me that her husband didn't really understand what it meant to be a Christian. She was concerned for both him and their children. She had a great desire to see them all in heaven one day.

The family attended our public launch service and became regular attenders. Soon, the husband came to understand the Gospel, turned from his sin, trusted Jesus to forgive him, guide him in life, and one day come back to take him to heaven. He then followed the Lord in believer's baptism. Over time each of the children also came to understand the Gospel, and each received the free gift of salvation through Jesus Christ.

Following my sermons each week, the congregation would stand to sing a song and I would extend an invitation for anyone in the room who had not yet trusted Jesus. I invited them to come to the front of the church and speak with me or another church leader about trusting Jesus. I also invited believers who needed prayer to come and allow us to pray with them about their needs.

One Sunday (a few years after the church began) as the invitation was given, I saw the mother of this family coming down the middle of the isle. I assumed she was coming to ask for prayer. However, she surprised me. She took me by the hand and said, "Pastor Mark, while you were preaching today, I realized that

I have never simply received God's free gift of eternal life. All these years I've trusted my good works to take me to heaven. I heard the Gospel, but somehow I thought it was for others. I thought if I tried really hard to be good enough, I could earn God's forgiveness and a place in heaven. But today I realized, I can't earn God's love; I don't deserve His forgiveness. He loves me and wants to forgive me, and He made that possible through what Jesus did for me when He died and rose again. Pastor Mark, today, I am turning from trusting myself and I am trusting Jesus Christ alone."

We prayed together that morning, and soon afterward she followed the Lord in true believer's baptism. Now, her family is complete. Each of them are members of God's forever family. One day, when the trumpet sounds, they will rise to meet Jesus in the air and so they will forever be with the Lord. They will enjoy eternity, not because any of them earned it or deserved it, but because of what Jesus did for them.

Like this lady, many today are trusting in their own good works to buy them a place in heaven. Paul was familiar with that vanity. When the resurrected Lord Jesus confronted him on the Damascus Road, he was working on his own 'self-righteousness project' (Acts 8:1-3; 9:1-9; 22:3-4). In fact, he thought he was succeeding.

Paul credited himself with an impeccable Jewish record: "Concerning the righteousness which is in the law, blameless" (Phil 3:6). But when Paul met Jesus he suddenly realized that everything he imagined was earning stellar brownie points with God was actually "rubbish" (Phil 3:8). He thought he was laying up treasures in heaven, but discovered he was only collecting garbage. He was shocked to learn his true status. All of his righteousness was filthy rags (Isa 64:6). He was the chief of sinners (1 Tim 1:15) rather than the most righteous Pharisee in Israel (Phil 3:4-6).

Paul addressed the 'law righteousness' crowd in the second clause of the explanation. "The strength of sin is the law" (1 Cor 15:56b). Do you think your law keeping, or religiosity, is your anti-venom for sin's snakebite? Guess again. "The law" which reveals sin only strengthens sin. The law makes sin more painful, poisonous, and potent. Rather than empowering us to obey God, it adds a sense of futility. The law reveals our sin nature's power and proclivity to rebel against God. It offers no remedy for rebellion.

Elsewhere Paul noted, "What shall we say then? *Is* the law sin? Certainly not!" The law is not the problem. The problem is inside you and me. Paul continued, "On the contrary, I would not have known sin except through the law. For I would not have known covetousness unless the law had said, *'You shall not covet'*" (Rom 7:7). The law shines its light on my sin, revealing my sin's true evil. Until confronted by the law, I thought coveting was my natural right. It sure felt right. "I Did It My Way," was my favorite song.

As Paul read the law, another strange thing happened within him. "But sin, taking opportunity by the commandment, produced in me all manner of evil desire" (Rom 7:8). That which the law reveals as wrong becomes an alluring temptation. I am attracted rather than repelled. When I see, "WET PAINT, DO NOT TOUCH," I desperately want to touch it. "For sin, taking occasion by the commandment, deceived me, and by it killed *me*" (v. 11). I end up with wet paint on my fingers; I receive the wages of sin that I earned—death. All of which leads to the ultimate question, "O wretched man that I am! Who will deliver me from this body of death?" (v. 24) Is there any hope or help for a wretch like me?

Remember the purpose of the explanation in Paul's brief digression. He wants us to understand just how great our total victory over sin and the grave will be when we are Raptured. We can summarize what we learned in our study of the explanation (1 Cor 15:56). Notice Paul's answer to his two questions (v. 55).

Question 1: "O Death, where is your sting?"

Answer 1: Inside me. "The sting of death is sin."

Question 2: O Hades, where is your victory?

Answer 2: Victory over sin, death, and the grave is not found in law keeping. Instead, "the strength of sin is the law."

So we are back to the question, is there any hope or help for a wretch like me? And by the way, what does all of this have to do with the rapture?

Thanksgiving

Paul's explanation would be hopelessly depressing if, second, he had not moved on to express thanksgiving. "But thanks be to God, who gives us the victory through our Lord Jesus Christ" (v. 57). Great news. Breathe a sigh of relief.

All human religions say, "Do." The biblical Gospel says, "Done."

Jesus won the victory for us. By His death on the cross "our Lord Jesus Christ" plucked out sin's stinger and sucked out its lethal poison. He "bore our sins in His own body on the tree" (1 Pt 2:24). He endured sin's pay, penalty, and poison. He, though sinless, suffered our curse and condemnation. Having shouted from the cross, "It is finished [Paid in Full]" (John 19:30), He commended His spirit into the Father's hands, hung His thorn-crowned head, and died.

The Lord Jesus Christ suffered death in our place. When He rose from the grave, He proved that He had conquered death and satisfied the Father's wrath against our sin. He alone, therefore, can give us victory over death. And He did it for all. Therefore, we who trust Him can say, "Christ has redeemed us from the curse of the law, having become a curse for us (for it is written, 'Cursed is everyone who hangs on a tree')" (Gal 3:13). Thus, Paul declared, "Therefore the law was our tutor to bring us to Christ, that we might be justified by faith" (v. 24). The law takes condemned guilty sinners by the hand and leads us to Christ, the only one who can justify us by faith.

Without Calvary, no one could overcome sin's "sting of death" or resist "the strength of sin" revealed by God's law. "But thanks be to God, who gives us the victory through our Lord Jesus Christ" (1 Cor 15:57). Without His resurrection, there would be no hope in the face of death and the grave. Yet, through His resurrection, we are assured that one day we too will rise (at the Rapture) and when we do, our victory will be complete. Death's sting will be finally overcome, the grave's hold will give way to ultimate, complete, and final victory.

Resurrection Hope Leads to Present Perseverance

At the Rapture, resurrection hope will be fully realized. Even though this hope is based in a future event, it can transform us today. It inspires perseverance, which is another present benefit of the Rapture. Paul noted, "Therefore, my beloved brethren, be steadfast, immovable, always abounding in the work of the Lord, knowing that your labor is not in vain in the Lord" (1 Cor 15:58).

Believers can persevere despite trials, despite persecution, and despite grief. We can persevere today because of what we know about the future. We know victory is coming. In fact, victory is assured. We know that one day Jesus will appear in the clouds with a shout, with the voice of the archangel, and with the trumpet of God. We know that in the twinkling of an eye moment, the dead in Christ will rise and we who are alive in Christ will be caught up together with them in the clouds to meet our Lord Jesus. We know that we will be transformed. We know that we will have resurrection bodies like unto Jesus's resurrected body. Knowing all of these amazing truths enables us to persevere today.

With an eye on future glory rather than the temporal grind, we can "be steadfast, immovable, always abounding in the work of the Lord" (1 Cor 15:58). I'm glad that no matter how difficult or long a trial may be, no trial is permanent. Eternal joy and bliss awaits every true believer. Today our Lord's work may bring great trial, but it will end in greater triumph. The trials may be vicious, but our work is not in vain (empty, meaningless). Today's reality may be hard, but tomorrow's reward will be heavenly. Therefore, since we know the Rapture is coming, we can persevere in following Jesus today.

> Paul concludes this tremendous theological discussion of the resurrection with a practical pastoral encouragement for the need for consistency and perseverance in our daily Christian lives. … It will be worth it all when we see Him and are welcomed into the eternal Kingdom![59]

Conclusion

Thus far we have considered two Scripture passages that speak directly of the Rapture of the church. Beginning with one of the clearest texts on the topic, we noted that 1 Thessalonians 4:13-18 uses the Greek word, *harpadzo*, translated, *caught up*. The Latin translation uses the word, *raptus*, which is the origin of our English word, *Rapture*. We noted, therefore, the claim that the New Testament does not teach the Rapture because the word is not in the Bible is indeed a spurious claim.

Next, we focused on 1 Corinthians 15:50-58. The passage connects the Rapture to the resurrection of Jesus Christ and to the future resurrection of all believers. All believers will receive resurrection bodies at the Rapture and therefore will qualify to inherit the Kingdom of God. Their resurrection hope will be fully realized at the Rapture of the church. The truth of the Rapture was a hidden mystery until God revealed it to His children through His New Testament revelation.

In the next chapter we will examine one more passage of Scripture that gives insight into the Rapture. The passage comes directly from the mouth of Jesusand was spoken to His followers on the night of His betrayal. Considering the historical and cultural context of His day, Jesus's words clearly describe additional information regarding the Rapture of His bride, the church.

5

Defending the Rapture
Part 3

My Father's House
John 14:1-6

While 1 Thessalonians 4 and 1 Corinthians 15 are the clearest statements about the Rapture, we will also consider one more passage. We look back from Paul's epistles to one of the most beloved passages in the book of John. It is a familiar passage, but perhaps you have not thought of it as a Rapture promise.

You are aware, of course, that the New Testament opens with the four gospels: Matthew, Mark, Luke, and John. These books tell the story of Jesus Christ's virgin birth (Matt 1:18-25; Lk 2:4-7), life and ministry on earth (Mk 1-15:16), and conclude with His death, burial, resurrection (Lk 23:26-24:49), His promise to return (Jn 21:22), and His ascension back to heaven (Lk 24:51). The four books are called "gospels" because they tell the "good news." Mark uses the word to mean, the "glad tidings" (Mark 1:1 DARBY) that Jesus Christ, the Messiah (Anointed One), the Prophet, Priest, and King promised by the Old Testament prophets, has finally come.

It will be helpful to note how our passage (John 14:1-6) fits into the flow of John's gospel. The Apostle John's presentation of the life and ministry of Jesus Christ follows a different pattern than do Matthew, Mark, and Luke, often called the "Synoptic[60] Gospels." They follow a largely chronological pattern and most of the recorded events are in all three books—they see things together. However, John presents our Lord's life in a more thematic fashion.

THE BROAD CONTEXT

Overview of John

John's introduction declares the eternality, Deity, and humanity of Jesus Christ, as well as the purpose of His incarnation (1:1-18). To fulfill his stated purpose for writing, John builds the next section of his book around 7 miracles and 7 related teaching times (1:19-12:50).

The events in John's first twelve chapters happened during the approximately three and one-half years of Jesus's public ministry. At chapter 13, John slows down and provides much more detail. Chapters

13-19 cover less than twenty-four hours. Chapters 13-16 begin with Jesus and his disciples in the upper room. They observe the Passover meal, Judas departs to betray Jesus, and Jesus warns, comforts, and teaches His faithful disciples. Next Jesus prays (17), is arrested and questioned (18), scourged, condemned, crucified, pronounced dead, and hurriedly buried in a new tomb (19).

John 20 jumps ahead to Jesus's resurrection on Sunday morning (vv. 1-18), a meeting with His disciples that Sunday evening (vv. 19-23), and His appearance at another Sunday evening gathering one week later (vv. 24-29). The chapter concludes with John stating his *Spirit-inspired purpose for writing a thematic gospel.* He said, "And truly Jesus did many other signs in the presence of His disciples, which are not written in this book;[61] but these [7 specific miracles] are written that you may believe that Jesus is the Christ, the Son of God, and that believing you may have life in His name" (vv. 20-31). John has two purposes in mind. He wants all of his readers to know and believe:

» Who Jesus is—the Christ, the Son of God.
» How to be saved—through faith in Jesus Christ.

Finally, John 21 concludes the book with a key event that sets the stage for the book of Acts. Jesus forgives and restores repentant Peter to fellowship, and re-commissions him (note especially vv. 15-19). As Acts opens, Peter is Spirit-filled and becomes the leading Apostle and personality in Acts 1-12.

THE NARROW CONTEXT

After overviewing John's gospel and considering his stated purpose, we are ready to focus our attention on the specific context of John 14:1-6. John 13 describes a few events in the upper room. Jesus celebrates the annual Passover meal with His twelve disciples in an upper room in Jerusalem (John 13:1). During the meal, He reveals that a betrayer is among them (vv. 18-30). Hearing this shocking news, all of the disciples doubt themselves, but no one suspects Judas Iscariot (Matt 26:20-22). He is one of the most trusted disciples; he is their treasurer and "had the money box" (John 13:29). Any donations given to Jesus's ministry are entrusted to Judas. No one, other than Jesus, knows he has stolen part of the money (John 12:6).

After the meal (John 13:2-3), Jesus gives His disciples a memorable final lesson about humble service. John leaves the description of Jesus instituting the Lord's Supper to the other Gospel writers,[62] but he alone tells of Jesus washing His disciples' feet (vv. 4-17).

That evening, following Judas's departure (v. 30), Jesus gives His final extended instructions to the remaining eleven apostles. His Upper Room Discourse is also known as "The Farewell Discourse" (John 13:31-16:33).[63] Jesus's teaching time is urgent. He knows He is within a few hours of His arrest in the Garden of Gethsemane.

Further, Jesus knows He will be betrayed, denied, tried, mocked, scourged, and then crucified for the sins of the world. He knows His body will be buried in a borrowed tomb and His fearful disciples will return to the upper room to hide. He understands their fear. He cares.

Jesus's last words were designed, not to criticize their weakness but to prepare them for what was coming in the next few days. He also had long-range plans. He prepared them to follow Him the rest of their days on earth.

THE IMMEDIATE CONTEXT

Now we zoom in further to note the immediate context of John 14:1-6—the concluding verses of John 13. After Judas leaves on his dastardly mission, Jesus tells the disciples that He is going away and they cannot now follow. But, in the meantime, they are to follow "a new commandment … love one another" (vv. 31-35). Peter, as usual, speaks up.

"Lord, where are you going? … Why can I not follow You now? I will lay down my life for Your sake" (13:36-37).

Jesus responds, "No, Peter. That's only wishful thinking. Before the sun rises tomorrow, you will deny Me three times" (see v. 38).

This must have rattled the apostles' cages. How could it be? If brash Peter can't remain faithful, who can? The shadow of despair is engulfing the room.

But to those shocking words, Jesus quickly adds, 14:1-6.

THE SPECIFIC TEXT

A Precept to Trust

Jesus began with a precept to trust, moved on to a promise of triumph, and concluded with a path to trod. The promise speaks of the Rapture of the church. Just as Paul did in 1 Thessalonians 4:18, Jesus offers comfort to His troubled disciples, and the comfort includes the Rapture.

Jesus said, "Let not your heart be troubled." Despite your fast approaching trials, including Peter's denials, "Believe in Me" (v. 1). They could trust Him because He is trustworthy, and so can we.

We may not understand our troubling trials any more than the disciples did that Passover evening. Events may come at us fast and furious. Yet, we can be assured that Jesus loves us and will never forsake us. We can trust His excellent plan.

A Promise of Triumph

Jesus moves from His trustworthy precept to a promise of triumph. He says, "In My Father's house are many mansions; if *it were* not *so*, I would have told you. I go to prepare a place for you. And if I go and prepare a place for you, I will come again and receive you to Myself; that where I am, *there* you may be also" (vv. 2–3). Certainly, these words are comforting to believers today. They gain even more significance when we see them in the light of a first century Hebrew wedding ceremony—specifically a Galilean wedding ceremony.[64] I do not believe the comparisons are coincidental.

A Bride Chosen

When a man decided he was ready to marry a certain young lady, he first discussed it with his father. If his dad agreed, the two of them opened a dialogue with the young lady's father. If her dad agreed to a proposal, the process moved to the next step.

In that day, a proposal was not a private event between the man and woman. Instead, a ceremony was held for the man to officially propose. Witnesses attending the ceremony included his family, the prospective bride's family, some friends, and some community witnesses.

The man made his official proposal by offering the young lady a cup of the fruit of the vine. The choice was then fully in her hands. If she rejected the proposal, she returned the cup without drinking. If she consented, she drank from the cup, returned it to him, and he also drank. He then pledged to her before the witnesses that he would not drink from the cup again until they drank it together at their wedding. With that, the gathered crowd broke into a happy celebration.

From that moment on, the couple was legally bound together as betrothed husband and wife. Unlike our modern engagements, a betrothal was legally binding. Only death or a legal divorce could break it. Normally, divorces were only granted if the bride or groom was found guilty of adultery.[65] Even so, the couple did not yet live together.

After the brief betrothal celebration, the man returned to his father's house. Under his father's watchful eye, the son prepared a place where he and his bride would live and establish their home. It might mean building a stand-alone house, remodeling a room in his father's house as a bridal chamber, or adding rooms to his father's house.

Once the son believed the place for his bride was prepared, he sought his father's approval. When his father agreed the work was complete and everything was ready, the son simply waited for his father's next directive.

A Bride Ready and Waiting

At the bride's home, everyone lived in anticipation. She made herself ready, preparing herself with beauty treatments. She also prepared clothes for the wedding, the wedding night, the wedding party, and for her new life with her husband. The bride, her family, nor their friends had any idea when the groom would return for her. Typically, it would be close to a year, but no one knew for sure. As time passed, everyone knew the groom's return was nearing. The bride lived in anticipation, knowing the groom could come for her at any moment, day or night.

Here Comes the Groom

Back at the groom's home, everything was ready. The bridal chamber was prepared and waiting. The son was going about his daily life and work, waiting for his father's command. The decision and timing were at his father's discretion. Finally, one wonderful day, his father gave the long anticipated directive, "Son, you may go and get your bride."

With great excitement and a shout, the groom, his family, and his close friends headed for the bride's house. Typically, a ram's horn was blown as the boisterous wedding party made its way through the streets. Laughter and shouts rang out. Soon the company gathered outside the bride's family home. The groom called for his bride to come and go with him to his father's house for their wedding celebration.

The bride emerged with her family and friends. Often, she sat on a litter chair. Four of the groom's friends lifted it onto their shoulders and transported her to the wedding celebration. The entire party of invited guests entered the father's house. The doors then were shut and secured. From that point on, no one else could enter. As the father and all the wedding guests began a seven-day feast, the groom took his bride to their wedding chamber to consummate their marriage.

The Upper Room

The first century Galilean wedding rituals are foreign to us in the twenty-first century. But they were familiar to Jesus and His eleven Galilean disciples.

The wedding rituals were a part of everyday life. As Jesus spoke, there is little doubt that a Jewish wedding immediately entered their minds. Grasping these facts sheds light on Jesus's statements for us today.[66]

Our Lord told His disciples that He was going away, but He would return for them. From other Scriptures, we know we are included. His bride—the church[67]—includes the eleven apostles and everyone who trusts in Jesus Christ as their Savior. Jesus promised to take His bride to His "Father's house" (John 14:2a). Like the betrothed husband, Jesus said, "I go to prepare a place for you. And if I go and prepare a place for you, I will come again and receive you to Myself; that where I am, there you may be also" (vv. 2b-3). This event is unique.[68]

In the upper room, Jesus did not focus on His future coming to judge the world. He will do that in due time,[69] but judgment is not the focus of this passage. Rather, Jesus focused on the joyful event when He comes for His bride.[70] Again, Scripture makes it clear that the church is the bride of Christ.[71] This is a word of comfort for all of Jesus's followers. We can hold to the promise that while He is gone, He is preparing a place for us in His Father's house.

Like a first century bride waiting on her groom, we know that every passing day brings us one day closer to our Lord's return. Now it is closer than it has ever been before. No one on earth knows when He will come; we just know He will come. Our knowledge is based on His faithful promises.

When everything is ready in His Father's house, the Groom's preparatory work will cease. From that point on He will simply wait for the Father's command. Be reassured. At just the right time, the Father will give the word. The Son will shout, Michael the archangel will shout, and Gabriel will blow the trumpet. Jesus will descend, the dead in Christ will rise and receive their resurrection bodies, and we who are alive and remain will be transformed and Raptured up to meet our Lord Jesus in the air. At our transformation, we too will receive resurrection bodies. Shouting and praising and celebrating Christ's victory over sin, death, and the grave, we will return to the Father's house for the Marriage Supper of the Lamb. What a day! What a day! What a day that will be!

Oh! Don't forget one more interesting fact consistent with the Jewish wedding practices of the first century. After Jesus took of the cup during the Last Supper and offered it to His followers, He said, "Assuredly, I say to you, I will no longer drink of the fruit of the vine until that day when I drink it new in the kingdom of God." (Mark 14:25) Each time we partake of the Lord's Supper today, we are reminded that Jesus is waiting to partake until He comes for His church and we enjoy the Marriage Supper of the Lamb. When we drink of the cup, it should not only remind us of Jesus's shed blood, but of His promise to catch us up to spend eternity with Him.

A Path to Trod

Jesus Christ's triumph is an exciting promise, but He did not stop there. He continued, "And where I go you know, and the way you know" (John 14:4).

These are familiar words. We love them. They comfort us. But don't breeze past this *pause-and-ponder* moment. You might miss Jesus's intended meaning.

The Apostles Knew

Jesus noted that the eleven knew *where He was going*. How did they know? He had just told them; He was going to the "Father's house." They also knew *why He was going*—to "prepare a place" for them. Further, they knew *the way to get there*—"the way you know" (v. 4). They even knew *when they were going*. Certainly, they didn't know the date on the calendar. But they knew the occasion. They would go to the Father's house when Jesus had everything prepared and returned to catch them up into His loving embrace. "And if I go and prepare a place for you," Jesus promised, "I will come again and receive you to Myself; that where I am, there you may be also" (John 14:3). A deeper, more personal, and more intimate relationship with Jesus than we have ever known awaits us in the Father's house.

The disciples knew *the path to trod*. They had followed Jesus on that path for almost three and a half years. No other pathway led to their desired destination. They knew all other paths led to other destinations.

The Narrow Gate

In the Sermon on the Mount, Jesus connected "the way" with another memorable metaphor. He described the entryway onto the path to life; it is in contrast to the path to destruction. "Enter by the narrow gate;" He said, "for wide is the gate and broad is the way that leads to destruction, and there are many who go in by it. Because narrow is the gate and difficult is the way which leads to life, and there are few who find it" (Matt 7:13-14). Destruction Blvd. is crowded. The entry gate is wide, easy to traverse, and popular. Lots of folks are headed that way. It is broad and inviting and can easily manage the congested traffic.

The disciples remembered the sermon. They knew how to pass through the gate and follow the path to the Father's house. He also told them which gate to enter.

Thomas's Question & Mine

Thomas, however, had a perplexed look on his face. The puzzle pieces weren't connecting for him. "Lord," he said, "we do not know where You are going, and how can we know the way?" (John 14:5).

Thomas didn't write a canonical gospel, but I'm very thankful he was among the apostles. His urgent question led to "the Light of the world" (John 8:12) revealing one of the most salient salvation statements in the gospels. It was the light I needed when I was searching in the darkness, and it is the light I have shared with literally hundreds of people across the years. "Jesus said to him, 'I am the way, the truth, and the life. No one comes to the Father except through Me'" (John 14:6).

ONE Among Many

There are many paths in life. All of these paths lead into eternity, but only one leads to the Father's house. All others lead to destruction because, "All have sinned and fall short of the glory of God" (Rom 3:23) and "The wages of sin is death" (Rom 6:23a). Even so, an obstacle blocks our passage. The narrow gate is locked.

Wide Gate & Broad Way

Sin is natural for all of us. Each of us inherited a fallen nature through our family lineage. Our fathers passed to us the sin nature they inherited from our grandfathers, who inherited it from our great-grand-fathers, who inherited a sin nature from our great-great-grandfather … all the way back to Adam, standing in the Garden of Eden chewing the first bite of forbidden fruit, while its juice trickled down his arm.[72] "Therefore, just as through one man [Adam] sin entered the world, and death through sin, and thus death spread to all men, because all sinned" (Rom 5:12).

The consequences of inherited sin are devastating. Because of our sin we neither deserve to go to the Father's house nor can we earn an entry ticket. We have earned death—separation from God in this life and for all eternity.

Yet, the Bible offers hope. God has intervened. Willingly, He sent His Son on a fatal rescue, redemption, and reconciliation mission. Through Christ, God has:

> [13] … delivered us from the power of darkness and conveyed [transferred] *us* into the kingdom of the Son of His love, [14] in whom we have redemption through His blood, the forgiveness of sins. …

[19] For it pleased *the Father that* in Him all the fullness should dwell, [20] and by Him to reconcile all things to Himself, … having made peace through the blood of His cross. [21] And you, who once were alienated and enemies … He has reconciled [22] in the body of His flesh through death, to present you holy, and blameless, and above reproach in His sight (Col 1:13-14, 19-22).

Therefore, "the gift of God is eternal life in Christ Jesus our Lord" (Rom 6:23b). He will take all believers to the Father's house where a happy wedding celebration will welcome our arrival. He alone can open the gate that leads to the way to the Father's house. He is both the "door" and the "way" (see John 10:9; 14:6).

In the upper room, Jesus prepared the eleven apostles for the approaching crisis. He knew what was coming. Within the next twenty-four hours He was betrayed by Judas, abandoned by His apostles, falsely accused, and condemned at an illegal Jewish show-trial. Pilate, the Roman governor, declared Him innocent no less than 3 times. Following the governor's verdict, He was violently scourged, unjustly condemned to death, and vicariously crucified.

On the cross our Lord Jesus finished His redemptive work. During His suffering, He saved one of the two thieves crucified beside Him, fulfilled Psalm 22 and Isaiah 53, committed His spirit to the Father, and hung His thorn-crowned head and died. Friends claimed His body to hastily bury Him before sundown.

On the morning of the third day after His death, angels came and rolled away the stone from His tomb door. Jesus rose from the dead, stood, stretched, and walked out of the tomb. Jesus Christ's bodily resurrection demonstrated that He had defeated sin, death, and the grave. He is alive forevermore.

In the upper room Jesus comforted His apostles. He knew they did not understand, even though He repeatedly forewarned them. He knew His suffering, death, and victory was coming. He reassured them that by turning from sin and trusting Him alone as Lord and Savior, they had entered the path to the Father's house. Even though they would face troubling times sooner than they imagined, He would not abandon them. At the Rapture, He would return and take them to the Father's house for the Marriage Supper of the Lamb.

Conclusion

These three passages (1 Cor 15; 1 Thess 4; John 14) reveal the Rapture of the church. If one believes in the inerrancy and infallibility of all Scripture, he is assured that the Rapture is a real *future event*.

The Rapture will be a *joyful event*. Every believer can look forward to it with hope and anticipation. We don't know when it will happen, but with every passing day it is closer than the day before. Be ready. Expect the shouts and the trumpet sound. When we hear them we'll look up to see Jesus in the clouds with nail-pierced hands outstretched. Suddenly, we'll be transformed and caught up. Our church family and believing loved ones and friends will be all around us. All the petty stuff will be forgotten. The aching knees and hurting hips will be gone. All the canes and walkers and wheelchairs and cancers and toothaches and psoriasis will be left behind. Together we'll join the shouting, going to meet Jesus. Just up ahead will be all the believers who were dead. They will have abandoned their graves and be on their way to glory. They will have traded ashes, dust, and decaying grave clothes for new, glorified bodies. They'll be shouting too. Jesus will receive us into His welcoming arms and take us to His Father's house. One moment we'll be here, and in the twinkling of an eye we will be there. I can't wait!

The three Scripture passages we have examined make it clear that the Rapture is promised, imminent, certain, and real. It will be personal; Jesus Christ will personally come for His regenerate church. When the Rapture occurs, it will be unexpected and sudden. Before we focus on answering the question on everyone's mind, "When will the Rapture happen?" we must examine a closely related preliminary issue—the distinction between the Rapture and Jesus's Second Coming to the earth. We now turn our attention to this important issue.

6

Distinguishing the
Rapture and the Return

Is the Rapture simply another name for the Second Coming of Jesus Christ? The answer is an End-Times 'bone of contention' stuck in many throats.

Those who believe the Scriptures teach a Pre-tribulation, Pre-millennial Rapture, believe it is a real event that will occur prior to a literal 7-year tribulation period. They believe the literal tribulation fulfills Daniel's prophecy of a future 70th Week (Dan 9:27). These interpreters believe the Rapture and the Second Coming are two separate events. Dwight Pentecost explained:

> This verse unveils what will occur in the 70th seven years. This seven-year period will begin after the Rapture of the church (which will consummate God's program

in this present Age). The 70th **"seven"** will continue till the return of Jesus Christ to the earth. Because Jesus said this will be a time of "great distress" (Matt. 24:21), this period is often called the Tribulation.[73]

Those who believe in a Partial Rapture, a Mid-tribulation Rapture, or a Pre-wrath Rapture also believe the two are separate events.

In contrast, those who believe Jesus Christ will return at the end of the tribulation (the Post-tribulation view) believe the Rapture and the Second Coming are the same event. Those who believe Jesus Christ will return at some point in the future, but do not believe in a literal tribulation or millennium (the amillennial view) likewise believe the Rapture and Second Coming are one event with two descriptive names.

I contend that the two events, the Rapture and Christ's Second Coming, are two literal events separated by earth's 7-year tribulation period.[74] The Rapture will be before the tribulation, and Christ's Second Coming will end the tribulation. Below, we will consider noteworthy distinctions between the two events. While I am not alone in my belief, a number of respected scholars defend the Post-tribulation Rapture view. As noted above, they believe the Rapture and the Second Coming are the same event. My concern, however, is the Biblical evidence, not which view is presently the most popular view.

Many writers note the differences between the Bible's descriptions of the Rapture and the Second Coming. If we take the Bible seriously, we cannot simply dismiss the distinctions; they are not insignificant. Hindson and Hitchcock, for example, note, "Similarities exist between the Rapture and the return, but the irreconcilable dissimilarities carry more weight."[75] They go on to describe ten specific distinctions, noting that these are but a few of the significant differences. Consider their list.

1. There is a difference in the signs given for each stage.
2. There is a difference in the place Christ will meet believers.
3. There is a difference in who removes people from the earth.
4. There is a difference in who gets taken from the earth and who is left.
5. There is a difference of when Jesus comes in relationship to the Tribulation.
6. There is a difference as to when judgment takes place.
7. There is a difference in the timing of the resurrection of the dead.
8. There is a difference in the people involved.

9. There is a difference in the mention of the Rapture of living believers.
10. There is a difference in the changes on earth associated with these events.[76]

Danny Akin formulated a chart of the distinctions between the two events. He notes 9 differences.

The Rapture	The Second Coming
Christ comes to receive His church in the air.	Christ returns with His bride and angels to the earth.
The seven-year tribulation begins shortly after the Rapture of the church.	The millennial kingdom (1,000 years) of Christ is established after the Second Coming.
The event is imminent; it could happen at any time.	Numerous signs precede this event (Rev. 6-19).
This is a message of comfort for believers.	This is a message of judgment (and warning) for unbelievers.
The church is of primary importance.	Israel is of significant importance.
The Rapture is a mystery.	The Second Coming is predicted in both the Old and New Testaments.

The judgment seat of Christ for believers occurs (Rom 14:10; 1 Cor 3:10-15; 2 Cor 5:10).	The sheep-and-goats judgment occurs (Matt 25:31-46); and the Antichrist and the world are judged (Rev 19:11-21).
Only believers are affected.	All people are affected.
The church is taken into the Lord's presence in heaven.	All believers are brought into the millennial kingdom to reign with Christ on earth.[77]

Akin, Hindson, and Hitchcock all point to reasonable and significant distinctions between the Rapture and the Second Coming. I too affirm each of the distinctions, but give some distinctions more weight than others. Note the following:

> 1.   At the *Rapture* the saints will be "caught up" to meet the Lord in the air. The dead in Christ will rise first, followed by all believers living at the moment of the Rapture (1 Thess 4:13-18). In contrast, at the *Return*, Jesus Christ will come to earth, escorted by both His saints and His angels (Rev 19:1-16).

2. At the *Rapture* the dead in Christ and the living who are in Christ will be snatched up from the earth in joy (1 Cor 15:54-57; Rev 19:6-8). At the *Return* those who reject Christ will be taken from the earth in judgment (Matt 24:40-44).

3. At the *Rapture* our Lord Jesus will return with a shout, with the voice of the archangel and the trumpet's sound. Believers will be taken from the earth to meet the Lord in the clouds. This is a comfort for pre-Rapture saints (1 Thess 4:13-18; 1 Cor 15:50-58). At the *Return*, with the sound of a trumpet, the Lord will send His angles to gather unbelievers from the earth for judgment. This is a warning for pre-Return sinners (Matt 24:29-31).

4. The *Rapture* is imminent. The entire New Testament from Acts 1:6-Revelation 22:20 emphasizes the expectation of the imminent Rapture. This imminence is often used to motivate believers in evangelism and faithful living (1 Cor 15:58). If Jesus could appear in the clouds at any moment, it is urgent that believers share the Gospel

and live an obedient lifestyle (1 John 3:2-3). Many warning signs precede the *Return.* (As a starting place, note Matt 24; Rev 6-19).

The New Testament uses similar terms to reveal the *Rapture* and the *Return.* At the same time, it gives different descriptions and notes the different outcomes of the two events. While I prefer to speak of two separate events, some speak of one event with two phases separated by a period of time. Either way, the evidence demonstrates that the *Rapture* and the *Return* are distinctly different events. One cannot conflate the two and reconcile the Biblical distinctions. Indeed, the Rapture takes place at a distinct moment in time and brings about different results than does the Second Coming.

What About the Signs?

There are no signs as to when Jesus will rapture the church. The *Rapture* is imminent; it may happen at any time—it is ready to take place. That fact warns all preachers, self-proclaimed "apostles" and "prophets," and all Bible students against setting a date for the Rapture. No one knows when it will happen.

In contrast, there are multiple signs of Christ's *Return.* These will appear after the *Rapture.*

How do we know?

Shortly before Judas betrayed Jesus, the apostles asked, "What *will be* the sign of Your coming, and of the end of the age?" (Matt 24:3). Jesus answered their questions. He revealed several disastrous judgments that will happen on earth before He returns in power and great glory to establish His earthly kingdom and to judge the people and nations of the world (Matt 24:4–25:46).

The first few weeks or months following the Rapture will witness multiple spiritual, political, financial, and natural disasters. These will occur as if in waves, one disaster upon another. They will include wars, rumors of wars, national clashes, regional conflicts, famines, and earthquakes—just to name a few. Prior to the revelation of the Antichrist, multiple false-messiahs will make matters worse. They will deceive many with false hopes, failed promises, and fatal reassurances. Despite widespread confusion and mass fatalities, these will be mere precursors, signs, or "birth pains" of far worse things to come.[78] As Craig Blomberg notes:

> Like a woman's contractions before her labor and delivery, these preliminary events remind one of the nearness and inevitability of Christ's return. But just as a woman may experience false labor and just as genuine

contractions still leave her uncertain about the exact time of delivery, so too the events of [Matt 24] vv. 4–8 do not enable us to predict the time of Christ's coming.[79]

The Bible reveals multiple events within the 7-year tribulation period's broad outline (Rev 4-19). As the tribulation progresses and God's dreadful, deadly judgments reveal both the stubborn rejection of His Son and His just wrath, all will not remain unrepentant. Multitudes of Jews and gentiles will repent of their sins, reject loyalty to the Antichrist, and receive the Lord Jesus Christ. But to the new believers living in the tribulation period, with the freshly clarified book of Revelation in their hands, Jesus said:

> "But of that day and hour no one knows, not even the angels of heaven, but My Father only. ... Watch therefore, for you do not know what hour your Lord is coming. ... Therefore you also be ready, for the Son of Man is coming at an hour you do not expect" (Matt 24:36, 42, 44).

If those living out the tribulation drama will not know the day and hour of Christ's *Return* to earth, we dare not claim to know the day and hour of the *Rap-*

ture. "Therefore you also be ready, for the Son of Man is coming at an hour you do not expect" (Luke 12:40).

Are You Ready?

From the perspective of heaven, Jesus Christ has gone to prepare a place for us. When all is ready, according to the Father's perfect will and timing, He will tell the Son, "Go and get your Bride." We who await the Rapture are to be sure we are ready to go. When the Lord appears, it will be too late to prepare. Are you ready?

Conclusion

This chapter concludes our five-chapter examination of the nature of the Rapture. Chapter 2 defined the Rapture and noted some who deny the Rapture. In chapters 3-5, we defended the Rapture, examining the three clearest 'Rapture texts' in the New Testament. Finally, in chapter 6, we noted specific distinctions between the *Rapture* of the church and the *Return* of Jesus Christ to earth.

Our discussion of the nature of the Rapture demonstrates that it is a real future event. We have not, however, considered the timing of the Rapture. Indeed, the three major Rapture texts (1 Thess 4:13-18;

1 Cor 15:50-58; John 14:1-6) affirm the reality of the Rapture, but other than indicating its imminence, and that it will occur when all things are prepared and the Father says, "Go," they reveal nothing else about the Rapture's timing.

A word of caution. We are not referring to the year, month, week, day, or hour. So, what do we have in mind? We now turn our attention to this vital debate.

Part 2
THE TIMING OF THE RAPTURE

7

The Post, Mid, Pre-Wrath, and Partial Rapture Views

When will the Rapture occur? The Bible gives no indication of a date we can log into our long-range planning calendars.

Even so, the timing of the Rapture is among the most divisive questions discussed among theologians, pastors, and people in the pews (or rows of chairs, as the case may be). It has sent multiple books to printing presses, inspired many heated discussions, broken long-term friendships, and split more than a few churches. These reasons alone demand a serious, careful, Biblical examination of the evidence.

Most Protestant pastors believe Jesus Christ will return in the future. However, when it comes to the timing of the Rapture, there is widespread disagreement.

As previously noted, LifeWay Research conducted an End-Times survey among 1000 Protestant pastors in 2016. One of the survey questions asked about the Rapture's timing. While 36% of the respondents affirmed their belief in a *Pre-Tribulation Rapture*, some 25% denied that the Rapture is a literal event. The next largest group, 18%, affirmed a *Post-Tribulation Rapture*. Four percent of the respondents affirmed a *Mid-Tribulation Rapture* view, and 4% agreed with the *Pre-Wrath Rapture* view. One percent claimed *Preterism*[80], and another 8% held some other view.[81] Even pastors differ on the timing of the Rapture. The differences are prominent, not only among pastors, but also among professors, theologians, and church attenders.

Danny Akin noted the five major views of the Rapture held by conservative evangelicals. Most of these views will be found in a large gathering of Baptists.[82] The five views include the:

» Post-Tribulation Rapture
» Mid-Tribulation Rapture
» Pre-wrath Rapture
» Partial Rapture
» Pre-Tribulation Rapture

Each view is described below. After brief descriptions of each, I will state why I believe the

Pre-Tribulation Rapture is the "blessed hope" clearly taught in Scripture.

The Post-Tribulation View

We begin by noting the view of the Rapture held by 18% of the LifeWay Research respondents.[83] For much of the last 50 years, those who rejected the pre-tribulation view often held this view. Douglas Moo, for example, argued for the Post-tribulation Rapture in the counterpoint book, *Three Views on the Rapture*.[84] Among conservative evangelicals, Moo is a respected New Testament scholar and has authored and co-authored numerous scholarly journal articles, books, and commentaries.

In the *Three Views* book, Moo defended his view and, with evident humility and respect, also responded to each of the other contributors. He concluded:

> The truth of the imminent coming of our Lord Jesus Christ is an important and indispensable element of biblical truth. That this coming is to be premillennial the Scriptures plainly state. That a time of unprecedented Tribulation will immediately precede that coming and the living believers will be Raptured into the presence of Christ at His

coming are also plainly stated. But the time of that Rapture with respect to the Tribulation is nowhere plainly stated. … What I think the Scriptures indicate about this relationship has been stated on the preceding pages. But … I cannot, indeed must not, allow this conviction to represent any kind of barrier to full relationships with others who hold differing convictions on this point.[85]

Moo's presentation is charitable. Nonetheless, he defends the post-tribulation view with vigor. He begins, "It is my purpose to present an exegetical and theological argument for the view that the church, or the saints of the present dispensation, will be Raptured *after* the Great Tribulation."[86] For those wishing to learn more about this view, Moo's chapter is a good place to begin.[87] On the other hand, to understand how one who believes the Pre-tribulation Rapture view respectfully responds to Moo's arguments, one can read Paul Feinberg's response in the same work.[88]

The pre and post-tribulation Rapture views agree that the 7-year Tribulation period is Daniel's 70th week and is yet future. The post-tribulation view holds that the Rapture will take place immediately following the Tribulation. Those who hold this view believe that Jesus will come in the clouds, gather up and transform the Church, resurrect the dead saints, then immediately return to earth with His saints, to establish His millennial (1,000-year) reign on earth.

THE MID-TRIBULATION VIEW

The Mid-tribulation Rapture has never had as many adherents as the Pre or Post-tribulation Rapture views. In LifeWay's survey, only 4% of the pastors affirmed this view.[89] However, a few significant scholars have held this position.

I have been privileged to learn from professors, pastors, and laymen alike. Through the years the Lord used many godly laymen and women to teach me invaluable lessons. Johnny V. Boley was one of those Baptist laymen. He served the Lord any way he could throughout his life. He was a bank employee by trade, but was also proficient in several languages—Greek, German, Spanish, Russian, Yiddish, and others. When I studied first year Greek, Johnny's tutelage proved invaluable. He loved the Lord, the Bible, and the Church, serving alongside several pastors, missionaries, and professors.

Just as I profited greatly from my dad's frequent discussions of various Biblical and theological issues, so I benefited from Boley's frequent and insightful theological discussions. However, though he was very interested, Johnny rarely discussed the Rapture. He tried to avoid conversations that typically produce more heat than light. Even so, I learned that the Pre-wrath position intrigued him.

Boley set out to settle the issue in his own mind once and for all. As a result of His diligent personal study, he wrote a small book, *Another Look at the Rapture*,[90] with a unique conclusion. Since he wrote to clarify his own thinking, he never tried to publish it. Maybe he preferred not to deal with friends becoming angry critics on a mission to correct his eschatology. I'm not sure. He did, however, share the manuscript with me.

Boley concluded that the Rapture would occur at the mid-point of Daniel's 70th Week. That, of course, is the conclusion of the Mid-tribulation view. However, his unusual conclusion was that the Tribulation would last three and a half years instead of seven years. He argues for what he calls a "Pre-tribulation, but Mid-week view."[91] His view of the Mid-Week Tribulation Rapture is not a common view.

Gleason Archer's chapter in *Three Views of the Rapture* explained the more common understanding of the Mid-tribulation Rapture. Archer asserted that the Rapture is taught in "1 Thessalonians 4 and related passages."[92] He then asked if the Rapture would occur prior to or immediately following the seven years of Tribulation. He answered, "Within the ranks of sincere Evangelicals, who believe in the inerrancy of Holy Scripture and the fulfillment of all biblical prophecy, there is a difference of opinion. There are energetic advocates of each interpretation. Between these two views there stands a third, the view that the Rapture will occur at the midway point between the beginning of the final seven-year period and its end."[93] Archer then dedicated thirty-one pages to defending his Mid-tribulation view.

The Pre-Wrath View

In 1990 Marvin Rosenthal proposed a newer view, arguing for a "pre-wrath" Rapture of the church.[94] He offered an alternative that renewed serious discussions of the Rapture's timing. While gaining some traction, Rosenthal's view did not gather a large following. Yet, it did garner enough influence to motivate a critique by Renald Showers in 2001.[95] By the time LifeWay Research conducted its 2016 survey, the view had reached a stable following from 4% of the pastors.[96] So what is the Pre-wrath Rapture view?

Showers's summary is helpful and accurate. The Pre-wrath Rapture view divides the 70th Week of Daniel into three time periods. These are:

1st   The birth pains (Matt 24:1-14); Seals 1-4 (Rev 6:1-8)

2nd The Great Tribulation (Matt 24:21); Seals 5-6 (Rev 6:9-7:17). The sixth seal is the precursor to the third period.

3rd The Day of the Lord, when God will pour out His wrath upon the earth.[97]

The Pre-wrath view declares that the Rapture and the Second Coming are the same event, and will occur "between the middle and end of the 70th week of Daniel 9 (perhaps about three-fourths of the way through the seven-year 70th week). ... [T]he church will go through the first half and a significant part of the second half of the 70th week before being removed from the earth."[98] Even though it teaches there will be only one "Second Coming or *parousia*," the Pre-wrath position suggests "Christ will come and go several times." In fact, "It teaches ... four future comings of Christ within the boundaries of the one Second Coming."[99]

Unlike the Post-tribulation view, this position holds that the church is Raptured out and taken to heaven prior to the opening of the seventh seal, which contains the seven trumpet and seven bowl judgments. Unlike the Mid-tribulation view, this view holds that the opening of the seventh seal takes place after the mid-point of the 70th Week. Those who hold this view believe that Jesus and the saints will return to earth to set up Christ's millennial reign at the conclusion of the bowl judgments.

THE PARTIAL-RAPTURE VIEW

The Partial-Rapture view had several proponents from the mid-nineteenth to at least the mid-twentieth centuries. John Walvoord, writing in the mid-twentieth century, noted, "There has arisen in the last century, … a small group of pretribulationalists who contend that only those who are faithful in the church will be Raptured or translated and the rest will either be Raptured sometime during the tribulation or at its end."[100] According to the Partial Rapture view, many of the believers initially left behind will grow in faithfulness and worthiness amidst their tribulation trials. A proponent explained, "The saints will be raptured in groups during the tribulation as they are prepared to go. … The basis of translation must be grace or reward. … We believe that frequent exhortations in the Scriptures to watch, to be faithful, to be ready for Christ's coming, to live Spirit-filled lives, all suggest that translation is a reward."[101]

Passages used to defend the Partial Rapture theory included Matthew 24:40-51; 25:13; Mark 13:33-37;

Luke 20:34-36; 21:36; Philippians 3:10-12; 1 Thessalonians 5:6; 2 Timothy 4:8; Titus 2:13; Hebrews 9:24-
28; Revelation 3:3; 12:1-6.[102] We can agree that these
passages urge believers to be ready and alert, faithful
and Spirit-filled, watching for our Lord's sudden, certain, and soon return. Faithful service is commendable.
However, not one of these 12 passages gives the slight-
est hint or nod toward a Partial Rapture.

The previously noted Rapture passages (John
14:1-6; 1 Cor 15:51-58; 1 Thess 4:13-18) are conspicu-
ously absent from the list; and, I suggest, there is a good
reason. None of the Rapture passages mention a Partial
Rapture, or a second, third, or fourth chance Rapture.
Instead, all three Rapture passages emphasize that every
believer will be caught up together. For example, "We
shall not **all** sleep [die], but we shall **all** be changed—
in a moment, in the twinkling of an eye, at the last
trumpet" (1 Cor 15:51-52). Not some now and others
later, but "**all** … in a moment" will be resurrected and
raptured. Also, "the dead in Christ" and those "who are
alive" in Christ "shall be caught up together … to meet
the Lord in the air. And thus we shall always be with
the Lord" (1 Thess 4:16-17).

Further, in His comforting response to Thomas, Jesus answered the Partial Rapture's question as to
'who' will be translated, and 'why' (John 14:1-6). Note
the context. Jesus and the Twelve observed their final

Passover together. The apostles needed His comfort because of His three shocking revelations.

First, Jesus revealed that a betrayer was among them (John 13:21-30). They couldn't believe it. Who could it be? Who would do such a thing?

Second, Jesus was going away, but they had to stay (John 13:31-36). Their remaining time together was short. "You will follow Me later," he reassured, "but not now." After following Him for three-plus years, this was a hard piece of matzo to choke down.

Third, Jesus warned that Peter would deny Him that very night. Peter protested, "No way, Lord. Not me. Not ever" (see John 13:37). But Jesus answered, "Most assuredly, I say to you, the rooster shall not crow till you have denied Me three times" (v. 38).

To all of this troubling news Jesus said, "Let not your heart be troubled; you believe in God, believe also in Me" (John 14:1). The verse is instructive. Notice the opening phrase, "Let not your heart be troubled." In the Greek text, "your" is plural and "heart" is singular. Jesus encouraged all of the apostles, personally and individually. Rather than urging them to be more faithful, Jesus encouraged their faith in God. He comforts troubled individuals.

Jesus reassured His apostles that He was going to the Father's house on a place-preparing mission (John 14:2). He promised a grand reunion when His mission is complete. "I will come again," He said, "and receive you to Myself; that where I am, there you may be also" (v. 3). Jesus added, "You know where I'm going, and you know the way to get there" (see v. 4).

Thomas was not so confident. He protested, "'Lord, we do not know where You are going, and how can we know the way?' Jesus said to him, 'I am the way, the truth, and the life. No one comes to the Father except through Me'" (John 14:5–6).

Do you see the contradiction of the partial Rapture teaching? The Rapture is not a reward for faithfulness. It is a glorious benefit of salvation by grace through faith in Jesus Christ. He is the one and only way to the Father's house. The Lord Jesus is the only access to the Father. He is the way, the truth, the life, the assurance of our redemption, resurrection, and Rapture—even for deniers and doubters like Peter and Thomas.

The question of whether or not the Bible supports the Partial Rapture view is more than a Rapture theory debate. The partial Rapture's defense reveals a deep theological flaw in its doctrine of salvation; it focuses on works rather than grace. We can also note the view's lack of distinction between the believing church and the professing church, as well as its overlooking the distinction between Israel and the church.[103]

We do not note the partial Rapture's lack of biblical support because the view has significant influence today. In fact, it does not. It did not have enough support to garner a separate category in LifeWay's end-times survey. We mention it because, as churches abandon biblical end-times instruction, believers increasingly are ill-equipped to recognize obvious errors. They are vulnerable when tired, old, and discredited views are resurrected as 'new' insights, discoveries, or revelations.

Having noted the Post-tribulation, Mid-tribulation, Pre-wrath, and Partial Rapture views, we now turn our attention to the Pre-tribulation Rapture view. I am excited to do so, because it is the view I hold. I believe the biblical evidence for the Pre-tribulation view of the Rapture is clear. We will begin with a summary of the view and a brief history of how the Pre-Tribulation view became the most popular Rapture view among evangelicals. We will then move to an overview of the biblical and theological defense for the view.

8

The
Pre-Tribulation View

THE RAPTURE

At any moment Jesus Christ could appear in the clouds with shouts and a trumpet call, to resurrect, transform, and Rapture His followers. That, in a nutshell, is the Pre-tribulation Rapture position. When the saints are caught up to meet the Lord in the air, Jesus Christ will personally take us to our eternal home.[104]

THE TRIBULATION

Immediately after the Rapture, the church will be in heaven. What will happen in heaven during the tribulation on earth? Several things.

We will stand before the Judgment Seat of Christ to receive rewards for our Spirit-empowered, Christ-honoring labors on earth (2 Cor 5:10). We will worship, bowing en masse around God's Throne (Rev 4:10-11; 5:8-12).[105] The scene will be a joy-infused celebration beyond all imagination. Each of us will enjoy our new, eternal, resurrection body and sin-free spirit. For the first time we will know unhindered personal intimacy with our Lord Jesus. We will give Him all the glory for our rewards. By His Spirit, He equipped, empowered, and enabled our worthy works. We will worship Him, casting our crowns at His feet (Rev 4:4, 10-11; 5:11-12). Finally, we the church, Christ's bride, will celebrate the Marriage Supper of the Lamb with Him (Rev 19:7-10).

At the Rapture, all those who are not in Christ by faith will be left behind. From a pre-tribulation understanding, what will happen on earth during the tribulation?

Those left behind will face a vastly different scene on earth. As the saints worship their Lord in heaven, Jesus Christ will receive and open a scroll that was sealed with 7 *seals*. The Bible describes the scroll and the only One found worthy to open it (Rev 5). The scroll contains the judgements of God reserved for the time of the seven-year Tribulation. As our Lord Jesus opens each royal seal, God will pour out His just wrath upon the earth and its inhabitants (Rev 6:1-8:6). Notice, God's wrath is being poured out from the opening of the first seal. The early judgments are not the wrath of the Antichrist as some suggest. These judgments come directly from the hand of Jesus—God the Son. He is the only one worthy to open the scroll. By the time the first six seal judgments are complete, one fourth of the world's population will have perished. Even so, the horrors will have only begun.

The *seventh seal* contains the 7 *trumpet judgments.* As each of the first six trumpets are blown, God's just wrath upon the earth intensifies (8:7-9:21). Wave upon wave of natural disasters, one upon another, will leave a polluted, burned, blighted, and bleak landscape. An additional one third of earth's population will die.

The *seventh trumpet* contains the 7 *bowl* judgements. As each bowl is poured out upon the earth, one after the other, the intensity of God's wrath reaches the greatest level of judgement in the entire history of the earth (Rev 15:1-16:21). Noxious infectious diseases and natural disasters will spread misery, destruction, and death throughout earth's surviving population. Their responses will reveal humanity's ultimate rejection and hatred of God (16:11).

As the 7 years of tribulation on earth conclude, Jesus will return to earth with His saints and His angels (Rev 17:1-19:19). This will be His Second Coming to earth. Jesus Christ will throw the Antichrist and the False Prophet into the lake of fire (19:20-21)). He will bind Satan for 1,000 years (20:1-3), and the ultimate fulfillment of the Davidic Covenant will begin (20:4-6; cf. 2 Sam 7:12-16; 1 Chron 17:10-14). Jesus Christ, King of Kings, and Lord of Lords, will rule and reign from His throne in Jerusalem for 1,000 years (Rev 20:6).

THE MOST POPULAR VIEW: HISTORICAL HIGHLIGHTS

As noted, among protestant pastors, the Pre-tribulation view is the most popular interpretation of the Rapture and the related end-times texts. How did this view gain its popular status?

Pulpits and Publications

I realize the following answer is an inadequate summary, but notice a few historical highlights of how Pre-tribulation Premillennialism became the most popular view. For example, in the late 1800s and early 1900s, current events such as the turn of the century and WWI created great renewed interest in prophecy. Men like D. L. Moody (1837-99) and C. I. Scofield

(1843-1921) popularized Pre-tribulation Premillennialism both nationally and internationally.

Moody's international preaching, along with
his US based schools and Bible Conferences, empha-
sized that Jesus Christ could return at any moment.
While Moody never focused on theological nuances,
he preached the imminent Rapture, and he preached
it often.

In the same era, Scofield's Study Bible appeared
in 1909 with its premillennial study notes. It gave pastors and laypeople an affordable, portable, single-vol-
ume tool for studying the entire Bible. It guided them
toward a consistent literal-grammatical-historical hermeneutic, which leads one to a Pre-tribulation Premillennial interpretation of the Bible. Many scholars,
whether in joy or sadness, have noted the vast influence
of the Scofield Study Bible.[106] Scofield's Dispensational theology, including the Pre-tribulation view of the
Rapture, influenced countless Baptists and evangelicals
through the years.

In the latter half of the twentieth century, the
mega-church movement in the US reached its zenith.
Among Southern Baptists, the pastors of these expan-
sive congregations were dynamic preachers, most were
also expository preachers, and nearly all, if not all, reg-
ularly, boldly, and urgently proclaimed the pre-tribulation Rapture of the church. The influence of these

pastors extended far beyond their congregations. Through their sermons at conventions, conferences, and through various media outlets, as well as in multiple books, pastors such as W. A. Criswell,[107] Adrian Roger,[108] and theological educator, Paige Patterson,[109] significantly influenced Baptists to embrace a Pre-tribulation Premillennial interpretation of the Bible.

In addition, prolific authors such as Harry A. Ironside, Charles C. Ryrie, John F. Walvoord, and J. Dwight Pentecost influenced countless Baptists and evangelicals. For example, through Ryrie's speaking at Bible conferences, teaching at Dallas Theological Seminary, and his many books and commentaries, including his systematic theology, *Basic Theology*, and in particular, *The Ryrie Study Bible*, he clarified Dispensational Premillennialism with its literal-grammatical-historical interpretation of Scripture.

The Pre-tribulation Rapture and the Tribulation Period were major themes in Evangelist Billy Graham's citywide crusades and nationwide primetime network television broadcasts. His preaching impacted millions across the USA, Canada, and Great Britain, as well as in multiple major cities of the world. From his first crusade in 1947 until his final sermon in 2005, Graham often preached about the Rapture. He declared that it is the only assurance that one can be with Jesus when the fearful Four Horsemen of the Apocalypse gallop out of prophecy and into reality. He often published these themes in his monthly *Decision* magazine and in his best-selling books, such as, *Approaching Hoofbeats: The Four Horsemen of the Apocalypse.*[110]

An aside that may interest only me, is that both Charles Ryrie and Billy Graham chose First Baptist Church, Dallas, as their home church and W. A. Criswell as their pastor.

Movies

In the 1970s a trilogy of end-times movies had a widespread influence among evangelicals, the American Church in general, and Baptists in particular. The first movie, *A Thief in the Night*,[111] was a dramatic depiction of the Pre-tribulation Rapture. Two sequels followed: *A Distant Thunder*[112] and *Image of the Beast*.[113] Both sequels warned of coming catastrophic events that will unfold after the Rapture in the 7 years of tribulation. The movies were shown in theaters, special event venues, and in churches. Those were fruitful evangelistic years, especially among the Baby Boomer generation. Thousands professed faith in Christ, fearing they would be left behind if Jesus returned that day.

These new believers swelled youth groups, and many were added to church roles as well. The impact on the churches and the nation's youth culture was undeniable. Even the national media acknowledged it. On June 21, 1971, "The Jesus Revolution" was the cover story of Time magazine. Among many other influences, the cover story noted the Rapture-fervor within this 'Jesus Revolution.' "For many, there exists a firm conviction that Jesus's Second Coming is literally at hand. Proclaiming the imminent end of the world and Last Judgment like so many dread, some millenarians [believers in Christ's future Millennial Kingdom] chart the signs of the Apocalypse with the aid of handbooks like *The Late Great Planet Earth*."[114]

Music

Music was another significant influence. Larry Norman's 1969 Album, "Upon This Rock," contained the track, *I Wish We'd All Been Ready*.[115] It was played on both Christian and secular radio stations across the nation, and was included in the movie soundtrack of *A Thief in the Night*. It became a staple in Christian concerts and was one of the first contemporary songs to be accepted as special music in local church services. The song remained popular throughout the 1970s and inspired many other songs with a similar theme.

Positives and Negatives

With all the emphasis on the Pre-tribulation Rapture, it is not difficult to understand how the view became prominent. However, the steady, regular drumbeat on the Rapture, especially in the decade of the 1970s, produced both positive and negative results.

On the *positive side*, countless individuals came to genuine personal faith in Jesus. In addition, many believers moved from being "nominal Christians" to becoming serious about their faith, seeking to stay spiritually ready to meet the Lord. They also became serious about evangelizing others.

On the *negative side*, some of the literature and sermons published and preached during the final two decades of the twentieth century tended toward sensationalism. Numbers of preachers, teachers, and self-proclaimed prophets made predictions about the Rapture and the end-times that moved far beyond Scripture.

In January of 1988, for example, a self-published book captured the attention of people across the United States. Edgar C. Whisenant's book, *88 Reasons*, explained how the Bible supposedly revealed the Rapture would happen in September 1988.[116] His 1989 follow-up book explained why it did not happen in 1988. He confessed that he had slightly miscalculated the Biblical evidence. "But now, 'trust me,' the calculations are correct." If memory serves, he declared there were 89 sure and certain reasons the Rapture would occur in 1989.

By 1990, Whisenant's false teaching was undeniable; no one was fooled—at least for a couple of decades. Then Harold Camping made the supposed amazing discovery, via biblical numerology, that the Judgment Day would begin with a massive earthquake on May 21, 2011. When that proved false, he updated his predictions to October 21, 2011.[117] Again, "Oops." And so it went for all the date-setters.

Obviously, none of the other predictions in the era were any more accurate. Jesus did not return on any of the variously predicted dates. Multiple unmaskings of the Antichrist, along with various identifications of the "mark of the beast," all proved false. These and other end-times claims went into the prophetic trash barrel because the Bible simply does not provide such details.

Growing Indifference

With each publicized false prediction, more and more people grew cold to the idea of a Pre-tribulation Rapture. Many became embarrassed to admit they were interested in the subject, much less willing to study and teach the end-times Scriptures. Many pastors stopped preaching the "blessed hope" and "comfort" of the church's imminent Rapture lest their church members think they had joined a lunatic fringe group.

Sensing that the biblical doctrine of the Rapture, and particularly the Pre-tribulation view, was waning, Tim LaHaye and Jerry B. Jenkins united to write a series of novels based on the Pre-tribulation Premillennial interpretation of the Bible. The *Left Behind* series gained a wide audience with 63 million+ copies sold.[118] Three movies based on the series further popularized the novels. LaHaye and Jenkins also published non-fiction works on the topic.[119] These influenced many, yet a significant number of believers remain skeptical.

As Hindson and Hitchcock note, "Every time there is a 'blood moon' or war heats up in the Middle East, there are a number of 'prophetic panhandlers' who assure us this is the Big One."[120] Following this statement, they offer a significant list of such predictions through the years. Each time predictions are made and proven false, skepticism grows. Hearts chill and people ask, "Where is the promise of His coming?" (See 2 Peter 3:1-7) Despite the many distractions, LifeWay's 2016 survey of protestant pastors across America found that 36% still believe the

Pre-tribulation Premillennial position best describes what the Bible teaches about the Rapture.[121] I was not a participant in LifeWay's research, but I too remain convinced that the Scriptures teach the Pre-tribulation Rapture. In fact, I will go on record defending the interpretation.

23 Reasons to Believe in the Pre-Tribulation Rapture

Nearly all Bible believing Christians agree that the Rapture will be an actual future event. The main disagreement is over the Rapture's timing. No Bible verse specifically states that the Rapture will occur just prior to Daniel's 70th week (the tribulation period). However, there are significant biblical, theological, and practical reasons to believe in the Pre-tribulation Rapture of the church. Consider the following.

Biblical Reasons to Believe in the Pre-Tribulation Rapture

1. Using a consistent literal-grammatical-historical interpretation of Scripture leads

one to expect the Pre-tribulation Rapture of the church. The trustworthy precedent, leading us to interpret prophecy literally, is the literal fulfillment of the Old Testament prophecies of Christ's first coming. The Old Testament prophets foretold many details about "His birth, His rearing, His ministry, His death, His resurrection … [and they] were all fulfilled literally."[122] Therefore, it is reasonable to expect all of the prophecies about His Second Coming to be fulfilled literally as well.

2. First Thessalonians 4:13-18 clearly teaches the Rapture is real, a source of comfort for the present, and a source of joyful hope for the future. At the Rapture:

   » Jesus Christ will appear in the clouds suddenly.
   » A shout and trumpet blast will resurrect the dead in Christ.
   » Both the resurrected and living believers will be caught up together to meet their Lord in the clouds.
   » Believers will always be with the Lord.

3.   First Corinthians 15:50–58 clearly teaches:

   » Both dead believers and living believers
      will receive glorified bodies at the Rapture.
   » Their glorified bodies will be like Jesus's
      resurrection body.
   » Only resurrection bodies can inherit the
      Kingdom of God. An earthly physical
      body simply will not do.

4.   John 14:1–6 clearly teaches:

   » Jesus went to His Father's house to
      prepare a place for His bride.
   » He promised to come again and receive
      believers unto Himself.
   » He promised to take His bride to the
      prepared place to be with Him.
   » Considering the historical description
      of the first-century Hebrew wedding
      practices, these promises are best fulfilled
      in the Pre-tribulation Rapture.
   » Faith in Jesus is the only way for anyone
      to become a part of Christ's bride.

5.   Jesus addressed the "churches" on earth 19
      times in Revelation 1–3. The church is not

mentioned again by name until Revelation 22, where Jesus returns His focus from the end times to our present age. He again addresses the "churches" (22:16) as they await His return. Jesus testifies to the churches that He is coming quickly (vv. 7, 12, 20). When He comes, He will reward those who understand Who He is and therefore trust Him fully and serve Him faithfully. Why is the church addressed only in its pre-tribulation existence, but never observed participating in the tribulation events on earth (Rev 4-18)? The pre-tribulation Rapture explains this fact clearly.

6. The "redeemed ... out of every tribe and tongue and people and nation" are in heaven worshiping Jesus (Rev 4-5). How did they all get there? The Pre-tribulation Rapture.

7. Though many people will place their faith in Jesus Christ during the tribulation, the primary work of evangelism is entrusted to the 144,000 Jews (Rev 7) and the two Jewish witnesses (Rev 11). The church is not mentioned as being on earth to participate during this time. Why are they not there

obeying the Great Commission? The simple answer is the Pre-tribulation Rapture.

8. At the beginning of Revelation 19, we observe the bride of Christ in heaven celebrating her marriage to the Lamb and enjoying the marriage supper of the Lamb. In the final half of the chapter the saints return to earth *with* Jesus, the Faithful, True, and righteous judge and warrior. The bride of Christ was in heaven to be married and to return with Jesus (Rev 19), that they might fill their assigned roles in Christ's millennial kingdom on earth (Rev 20). How did the bride get to the wedding feast? The Pre-tribulation Rapture.

9. The Pre-tribulation Rapture fits the New Testament references to the church being a mystery and makes sense of the time gap between the 69th and 70th weeks of Daniel (Dan 9:24-27). In the Old Testament era, which included Daniel's weeks 1-69,[123] God primarily witnessed to the world through believing Israel. In the Tribulation Period (Daniel's 70th week), God's focus will again be on Israel. Through the 144,000 Jewish

evangelists and the 2 witnesses, multitudes will turn to Christ (Rom 11:25-27; Rev 7:9, 13-14)), and they will do so despite persecution and martyrdom (Rev 6:9-11). In those days, Israel will recognize the longed-for Messiah is none other than Jesus Christ whom they rejected and crucified (Zech 12:10). They will mourn, repent, and confess (Isa 53:4-6) Jesus as their Messiah, Lord, and King. But in the present era God is primarily working through the church. The Church was a mystery because it was not identified in the Old Testament and because it includes Jews and gentiles united as equals in a loving family (Eph 2-3)— brothers and sisters in Christ.

10. We see a clear distinction between passages that speak of the Rapture, where Jesus Christ comes in the clouds and believers are "caught up," versus passages that speak of the Second Coming where Jesus comes and physically returns to the earth.

11. God's wrath will be poured out on the earth during the tribulation period (Rev 6:15-17; 14:19).

12. Jesus promised to deliver the church from the coming wrath of God (1 Thess 1:9-10; 5:9; Rev 3:10; see Rom 8:1).

13. The Bible exhorts the church to look for Christ, not the Antichrist (Titus 2:13-14).

Theological Reasons to Believe in the Pre-Tribulation Rapture

1. *The imminent return of Christ* – The early church was unanimous in believing Jesus could return at any moment. This is only possible in three scenarios:

   » Pre-Tribulation Rapture
   » Partial-Rapture
   » Amillennial Rapture

   Both the Partial-Rapture and the Amillennial positions are inherently filled with insurmountable hermeneutical and theological problems. Therefore, the imminence of Jesus's return points to the Pre-tribulation Rapture.

2. While believers in the church age experience God's discipline (Heb 12:5-8) and will

certainly experience Satanically inspired persecution and tribulation (John 16:33), *the church will never experience God's wrath and condemnation* (Rom 2:5; 8:1). Jesus paid it all. He promised to deliver the church from the coming wrath of God (1 Thess 1:9-10; 5:9; Rev 3:10). A literal grammatical reading of Revelation 4-19, which takes figurative language into account, demonstrates that Jesus Christ alone is worthy to open the scroll (5:1-7). As He does, God's wrath is poured out on the earth and its inhabitants (Rev 6:16-17). Were the church present to endure God's wrath, God would be unfaithful to His repeated promises. But that is impossible because God cannot lie (Titus 1:2). He will not fail; He will keep every one of His promises.

3. The Church is Christ's bride and Jesus is the perfect, faithful, loving bridegroom (Eph. 5:33). Why would He beat, abuse, and even behead His bride before the wedding and marriage supper? Rather, He "nourishes and cherishes it" (Eph. 5:29).[124]

4. There is *a clear distinction between the nation of Israel and the Church*. Romans 9-11 make it clear that God is not finished with Israel. Salvation has always been by grace alone through faith alone (Eph 2:8-9; cf. Heb 11). All Jews and gentiles were and are saved by Jesus Christ alone (Acts 4:12). God sent the message of salvation and has dealt with the world in different ways during different eras of history. In the Old Testament He dealt with the world primarily through the nation of Israel. Today God is dealing with the world primarily through the Church.

5. *Daniel prophesied 70 weeks* [1 week, 7 days = 7 years] *in which God would deal with the world through the nation of Israel*. The first 69 weeks concluded with the cutting off of the Messiah (Dan 9:24-26a). This prophecy was fulfilled in history. Since Jesus ascended and sent the Holy Spirit (Acts 2), God has dealt with the world through His Scripture-guided, Spirit-empowered churches. Yet, one week remains – one period of 7 years— in which God will once again deal with the world through the nation of Israel. At the Rapture the church age will be complete,

the Anti-Christ will rise and make a 7-year peace treaty with Israel, allow them to rebuild the temple, and the 70th week of Daniel will begin to be fulfilled (Dan 9:26b-27). *The main purpose of the tribulation is to bring the nation of Israel to faith in Jesus Christ* (Rom 11:1, 11, 25-29). Since the church is not in the first 69 weeks, we have no reason to expect the church to be in the 70th week.[125] The Pre-tribulation Rapture of the church is the best way to understand the fulfillment of Daniel's prophecy of the 70th week.

Practical Reasons to Believe in the Pre-Tribulation Rapture

1. The Pre-tribulation Rapture provides a time and place for the Judgment Seat of Christ (2 Cor 5:10; 1 Cor 3:12-15).

2. The Pre-tribulation Rapture provides a time, place, and bride for the Marriage and Marriage Supper of the Lamb (Rev 19:9).

3. Though God can do anything He wills to do, the Pre-tribulation Rapture answers the question of how believers can be "caught

up" in the clouds, eat the Marriage Supper of the Lamb, receive their rewards at Christ's Judgment Seat, and return to the earth "in a moment, in the twinkling of an eye" (1 Cor 15:52).

4. The Pre-tribulation Rapture explains how the earth will be populated with non-glorified humans during the Millennial Kingdom, and Christ and His glorified saints will rule over them. Those who are saved and manage to survive the tribulation will be set apart at the Judgment of the nations, and will be allowed to enter Christ's Millennial Kingdom (Matt 25:31-46).

5. The Pre-tribulation Rapture provides the opportunity for children to be born during the millennial reign, and accounts for the presence of unbelievers in the millennium who will join the rebellion when Satan is released for a short time (Rev 20:7-10).

I am convinced the Rapture will take place prior to the start of the 7 years of Tribulation on earth. Even if you aren't convinced, one thing is certain. No matter what one holds about the timing of the Rapture, anyone who takes the Bible seriously must acknowledge the reality of the Rapture.

Summary

We acknowledge that while Baptists and other conservative evangelicals widely accept the reality of the Rapture, there is disagreement and controversy over the timing of the Rapture. We noted the five most prominent views of the Rapture's timing, and briefly defined each position. We suggested a few reasons the Pre-tribulation view became and has remained the most popular interpretation for more than one hundred years. Abuses by some who claimed this position were acknowledged. We then considered 23 reasons to believe in the Pre-tribulation Rapture. We now turn our attention to a somewhat controversial question, "Does the Rapture Still Matter?"

9

Does the Rapture Still Matter?

A growing number of pastors, professors, and churches now answer this chapter's title with a resounding, "No." These friends prefer to avoid eschatological discussions and focus on Christian living for today. I too believe in developing faith-filled disciples. I'm thankful for those who faithfully win and disciple new believers. But I disagree that discipleship excludes eschatology. Teaching and preaching about the Rapture is not a hindrance to or a distraction from growing in grace. I am convinced the opposite is true.

The Bible's clear teaching about the Rapture is vital. It matters now more than ever. We are closer to the Rapture than we have ever been. And we'll be even closer tomorrow. If I were not convinced of that fact, I would not have taken the time to write this book.

Christian Living 101

Paul was not teaching PhD seminars when he wrote to his friends in Thessalonica and Corinth. He was teaching Christian Living 101. These were new churches filled with new converts. Most had only recently turned from false gods and pagan idols to Christ (1 Thess 1:9-10). Yet, to these very people, Paul declared the Rapture and the Second Coming.

The Rapture is vital; it is part of the basics for new believers. It is not, as is often assumed today, a private discussion reserved for moldy academics with nothing better to speculate about. It is basic Christian truth. The Rapture—rightly understood—is hope, comfort, and inspiration for living a vibrant Christian life today.

The Rapture still matters. In fact, it matters to at least two groups of people.

The Unforgiven

First, the Rapture still matters to those who have not yet turned from their sin and trusted Jesus Christ alone for salvation. How about you?

If it is true that Jesus could return at any moment and take all who trust Him to a joyful reunion at His

Father's House, nothing is more important than being ready to go when He comes.

Are you sure you are ready? If not, you will be left behind.

The Rapture matters to everyone who is not saved. That includes you—realize it or not, like it or not. But here is the good news: you still have time. Please don't waste it. Don't delay. Turn to Jesus today. The Rapture still matters because it is closer than you think.

The Forgiven

Second, the Rapture still matters to those who have turned from their sin and trusted Jesus Christ. *It matters as we witness.*

Coupled with the Gospel, *the Rapture is a sobering and compassionate invitation.* Certainly, we should avoid manipulation and wild speculation. We can trust God to work as we stick to Biblical truth. The Gospel is still "the power of God to salvation for everyone who believes" (Rom 1:16). Yet, there is nothing wrong with telling unsaved friends that while we are waiting "for His Son from heaven," we are urging all who will listen to be delivered "from the wrath to come" (1 Thess 1:10). God's wrath is sobering. Directing people onto the path to escape from God's wrath (John 14:6) is compassionate.

The Rapture is an evangelistic motivation. It motivates us to witness to our loved ones while there is time. "Therefore, my beloved brethren, [since at any 'moment, in the twinkling of an eye, … the trumpet' will 'sound' (1 Cor 15:52)] be steadfast, immovable, always abounding in the work of the Lord, knowing that your labor is not in vain in the Lord" (1 Cor 15:58).

The Rapture also matters in daily Christian living. Everyone, forgiven or unforgiven, faces heart troubling times (John 14:1). No one escapes troubles in this life. It is part of living in a fallen world. The closer we get to the Rapture; the more troubling times will increase. Add the end-times "birth pains" (Matt 24:6-8) to the sicknesses and sorrows of life, and it is easy to let Christ's promised "peace" (John 14:27) slip through our fingers. Yet, if we trust the Scriptures, when the world around us appears to be falling apart, we can be confident that everything is, in fact, falling into place.

So what does that have to with the Rapture? Lots.

Jesus said to His troubled apostles, "Let not your heart be troubled." What will take away the troubles? Faith in the Son and His sure promise, "I go to prepare a place for you. And if I go … I will come again and receive you to Myself" (John 14:1-3). Likewise, Paul described the Rapture to confused and grieving new believers. He concluded, "Therefore comfort one another with these words" (1 Thess 4:18).

Jesus is preparing our place.

He is certain to return.

Until He comes, comfort one another with this fact.

For these reasons and more, to the forgiven and unforgiven (and that's the only kinds of people there are), the Rapture still matters.

Appendix

How to Be Sure You Won't Be Left Behind

Understanding what the Bible teaches about the Rapture affects different people in different ways. For example, it gives great comfort to some. I've experienced that. Some, however, see the Bible's clear message about the Rapture and feel overwhelming shame. I've witnessed that. For still others, the Rapture is a source of great fear. Why the different responses?

Great Comfort

The day my mother died the reality of the Rapture brought me great comfort. I was sixteen years old and had worked in the sound booth at our church's Sunday night service. As I drove home on that pleasant Pueblo,

Colorado, evening, I was thinking about the shocking reminder Pastor Spannagel had shared. He said, "When we left church last Sunday, none of us expected that Coach Larry Marchbanks would suddenly die of a heart attack on the baseball field." He was right. The teacher, football coach, and member of our church was only 24 years old. He appeared to be in the prime of life and best of health. Naturally that was on my mind, but it never occurred to me that I was about to hear even more shocking news.

I parked the car, planning to be home for the evening, but my brother-in-law surprised me at the door. "Mark," he said, "you better head to the hospital. Your mom was rushed to the hospital a little while ago. I'm not sure what's wrong." I ran back to the car, praying as I drove across town.

It was June 3, 1984. Since we had no cell phones, I had no idea what to expect. Upon arriving I learned that my mother was fighting for her life. As evening turned into night, she grew steadily weaker. Her doctor gave us little hope.

In the early hours of Monday, June 4, 1984, I returned to the waiting room after my turn at mother's ICU bedside. I realized I was not likely to see her alive again.

Several members of my family and my pastor looked up. I knew their question. "No change," I said.

I sat down but looked up to the Lord for comfort. He brought 1 Thessalonians 4:13-18 to my mind.

I found it in my pocket New Testament and wanted to read it aloud. I knew I couldn't without choking up, so I handed my Bible to my pastor. He read those powerful, reassuring words to our sorrowing family. Knowing Mother's death was imminent brought us great grief. But, at the same time, the promise of the imminent Rapture brought us great relief.

That night we were reassured; we were not saying, "Goodbye." We were saying, "See you at the Rapture." Knowing the Rapture can happen at any moment gives great joy and comfort to believers, even in our trials and sorrows and tears.

GREAT SHAME

So why do some feel shame? Once after preaching about the Rapture, a friend approached me. He said something striking. "Pastor Mark, I'm not afraid for Jesus to come back. I know that He has forgiven me of my sins, and I have a home in heaven. If he comes back right now, I'll go to live with Him for all eternity. But Pastor, if Jesus came back today, I would be ashamed to see Him. For the past few months, I haven't been living for Jesus. I've been focused on myself."

I listened to my friend and encouraged him to confess his sin to Jesus. I reminded him of God's faithful promise, "If we confess our sins, He is faithful and just to forgive us of our sins and cleanse us from all unrighteousness" (1 John 1:9). Isn't that good news? He is faithful, even when we are not.

That day, my friend confessed his sin to Jesus, received His forgiveness, and renewed his close walk with our Lord. Immediately, his heart was filled with peace, the joy of forgiven sins, and the comfort of the imminent Rapture. First John 3:2-3 was confirmed in my friend's life.

GREAT FEAR

While the fact that the Rapture could happen at any moment brings some people comfort and others shame, still others live in fear of the Rapture. Many years ago, my wife and I planted a church in Dallas, Texas. The Lord has allowed us to be a part of several church plants, but that was the first.

Scott, a musically talented young man, began attending the new church. When I discovered his exceptional talent, I enlisted him to play the guitar for our services.

One Sunday, the Lord led me to preach about the Rapture and to emphasize that Jesus could return for His children at any moment. Throughout the sermon

I could see that Scott was disturbed. He couldn't hide it. After the service ended, I noticed Scott hung around longer than usual. I suspected he wanted to talk. So, I waited, making myself available. Finally, he mustered the courage.

Scott walked up to me and said, "Mark, when do you think Jesus is coming back to Rapture His church?"

"No one knows the day nor the hour," I said.

"Yeah, yeah, but do you really think it could be soon?"

Scott had a rough exterior. He didn't appear to be afraid of anyone or anything. In fact, it was difficult for Scott to be vulnerable and allow me to see the crack in his armor. He didn't want to admit his great fear that Jesus might actually return for His people that day. Still, he realized it was too urgent to let pride stand in his way.

"Mark, I'm not ready for Jesus to return. I've been listening to you. I understand I'm a sinner and can't save myself. The only way I can be sure my sins are forgiven and I have eternal life, is if I trust Jesus to be my Lord and Savior. I get it. I plan to do that someday, but not yet. Right now I have some things I want to do that He would consider worldly. Today's sermon hit me hard. If Jesus came back right now, I'd be left behind!"

How About You?

Do you know for certain that if Jesus appeared right now, you would be caught up to meet Him in the air? Would you be in the crowd going to His Father's house? Are you sure you would be "caught up to meet Him in the clouds and forever be with the Lord?"

If so, great!

If not, I have some good news for you.

Bad News…

Yet, the good news begins with some bad news. Like a diamond displayed by a jeweler, the bad news is the dark background that helps us see how good the good news really is. The foreboding reality is, "All have sinned and come short of the glory of God" (Rom 3:23). God created us in His image and likeness. He made us for a deep, intimate, personal fellowship with Him. He wants to connect with you and me on a deep, personal level.

Even so, we have resisted Him and rejected Him. Our sin gums up the works. Sin pushes us away from God and onto a road headed downhill, away from God.

God is *holy*. He is very different from us. He does not sin and is not tempted by sin. Nothing in His character and nature attracts Him to sin. Isn't that very different from us?

Further, God is *just*. He will judge everyone by the same standard. Therefore, He must punish our sin as surely as He must punish Hitler's sin.

Having said that, your situation, while dire, is not hopeless. You have not gone too far and fallen too deep into sin for God to reach you. Nor is God hard of hearing. Isaiah said, "Behold, the LORD's hand is not shortened, that it cannot save; nor His ear heavy, that it cannot hear" (Isa 59:1). At this point you may be asking, "So, what's the problem? If God thinks I need to be rescued, and He can do it, why doesn't He? Shouldn't God get with the program?"

Those are fair questions, and Isaiah has a simple answer. God is not the problem. What is? "But your iniquities have separated you from your God; and your sins have hidden His face from you, so that He will not hear" (Isa 59:2). Though God made us for fellowship and desires a relationship with us, our sinful choices erected a barrier between God and us. We put a short in the communication line.

Not only have we all sinned, but the Bible is also clear that "the wages of sin is death" (Rom 6:23). Sinful choices have consequences—death and separation from God. If Jesus returns or if you die with the sin barrier between God and you, you will be separated from Him eternally.

Good News…

Despite the bad news, let's rush to the good news. In fact, it is great news! While God is holy and just and therefore must punish our sin, He also is loving, merciful, and gracious. He made a way for all of our sins to be forgiven. He did everything necessary to remove the sin barrier and repair the short in the communication lines. In fact, that is why Jesus came to earth the first time.

Jesus is the eternal Son of God. He left heaven, was conceived in a virgin's womb, and 9 months later was born as a human baby. You've heard the Christmas story, but don't miss the Christmas miracle. God took on human flesh. He walked through life, experiencing the ups and downs of living in this world. In fact, the Bible says, "He was tempted in all points like as we are, yet without sin" (Heb 4:15). Jesus Christ was 100% man. Therefore, He faced temptation. He was also 100% God; therefore He never sinned. These two realities made it possible for Jesus Christ to be our substitute.

The Bible tells us, "All we like sheep have gone astray; we have turned, everyone, to his own way; but the LORD [God the Father] has laid on Him [God the Son] the sin of us all" (Isa 53:6). When Jesus suffered and died on the cross, He endured all of the necessary punishment for my sin and for yours. He suffered God's justified wrath against our sin.

In short, the price for your sin has been paid. In fact, just before Jesus died, He cried out, "Paid in full" (John 19:30). Some translations say, "It is finished." The Greek word is *tetelestai*. Most often this word was used to describe a debt that was finally paid off. *Tetelestai* was written on ancient payment receipts—paid in full.

Jesus declared that your sin debt was paid. On the cross, He made your payment in full. He did everything necessary to retire your sin debt in full.

The good news doesn't stop there. Not only did Jesus die in your place, but He also defeated sin, death, and even the grave. Three days after He died, Jesus rose from the grave! He defeated sin and overcame death. He won the victory by physically coming back to life and receiving a new glorified body (1 Corinthians 15). He sat up in the tomb where His dead body had been for 3 days. He stretched, stood, and stepped out of the tomb, alive and well for evermore.

Over the next 40 days, He appeared to His half-brother James, Peter and all the Apostles, and no less than 500 other eyewitnesses. He even had personal conversations and teaching times with many of them (1 Cor 15:5-7). He commissioned the Apostles to lead the churches in taking the gospel to the whole world (Matt 28:18-20), and then He ascended to heaven (Acts 1:8-11).

Your Response…

Today, Jesus is seated at the right hand of the Father in heaven. He is now offering you forgiveness of sin, a real relationship with Him, and the absolute assurance that one day you will spend eternity with Him.

Notice what I wrote. "He offers…" Jesus's offer stands, but you must receive the offer for His death to be applied to your debt account. The Bible says, "If you confess with your mouth the Lord Jesus and believe in your heart that God has raised Him from the dead, you will be saved. For with the heart one believes unto righteousness, and with the mouth confession is made unto salvation" (Rom 10:9-10).

In another place, Jesus says, "He who believes in Me has everlasting life" (John 6:47). To believe means "to trust." You must turn from your sin and from trusting in your own ability to be good. You must turn to Jesus, believing that He is the Son of God who died in your place, that He paid your sin debt in full, and that He arose from the dead. Trust Him and Him alone to forgive you, come into your life, to lead you now and give you an eternal home with Him when you die or when He Raptures the church.

Paul added, "For whoever calls on the name of the LORD shall be saved" (Rom 10:13). Prayer is one way to express your faith in Jesus. Call on Him. Tell

Him you are a sinner. Thank Him for paying the debt you owed. Ask Him to be your Savior, to be your Lord, to take over your life, to cleanse all of your sin, and empower you to live to please Him. Express the desire of your heart in your own words. No need to be eloquent; just be honest. He will hear, the barrier will crumble, and you will be a child of God.

As we learned from Romans 10:9-10 above, once you believe in your heart, you should "confess with your mouth." You should stop right now and call another believer. Maybe it is a parent, a child, a friend, but you should call or text someone right now and tell them that you have trusted your life to Jesus.

If you have done that for the first time, we would like to know it. Please email us at: m.ballard@nebcvt.org. We will rejoice with you and help connect you to someone in your area who can help you in your new walk with Jesus.

Oh! One more piece of good news. If you have trusted Jesus as your Lord and Savior today, you never have to fear the Rapture. When Jesus comes in the clouds, the trumpet sounds, and Michael shouts, you will be "caught up to meet the Lord in the air, and so you will always be with the Lord" (1 Thess 4:17). You will not be left behind!

ENDNOTES

1. Tim LaHaye and Ed Hindson, "Introduction" in *Exploring Bible Prophecy from Genesis to Revelation*, Tim LaHaye and Ed Hindson, gen. eds. (Eugene, OR: Harvest House Publishers, 2006), 7.

2. LaHaye and Hindson, *Exploring Bible Prophecy*, 7.

3. Mark Hitchcock, *Can We Still Believe in the Rapture?* (Eugene, OR: Harvest House Publishers, 2017), Kindle Location, 1046.

4. "Belief in the Rapture," *Lifeway Research*, accessed September 11, 2021; https://lifewayresearch.com/search/Belief in the Rapture/.

5. "Eschatology" is a study of the End Times.

6. Hitchcock, *Can We Still Believe in the Rapture?*, Kindle Location 667.

7. Charles Caldwell Ryrie, *Basic Theology* (Wheaton, Ill: Victor Books, 1986).

8. William R Kimball, *The Rapture, a Question of Timing* (Grand Rapids, Mich.: Baker Book House, 1985).

9. Paige Patterson, Revelation, in *The New American Commentary*, vol. 39, gen. ed., David S. Dockery (Nashville: B&H Publishing, 2012), 150.

10. Mark Hitchcock, *Could the Rapture Happen Today?* (Sisters, Or: Multnomah Publishers, 2005).

11. Ibid., 58.

12. Ibid., 57-59.

13. Ibid., 60-61.

14. Cecil Maranville, "The Rapture: A Popular but False Doctrine," Text, *United Church of God,* last modified August 1,

2008, accessed September 6, 2021, https://www.ucg.org/world-news-and-prophecy/the-Rapture-a-popular-but-false-doctrine.

15. Erickson and Grudem both argue in their respective systematic theologies that the pre-tribulation Rapture is a recent concept and attribute the idea to John Nelson Darby (1800-1882). However, as noted in the paragraph above, Gumerlock has clearly demonstrated that there were indeed advocates of a pre-tribulation Rapture dating back to at least the eleventh century. To have a better understanding of Erickson and Grudem's discussions, see: Erickson, Christian Theology, 3rd ed., 1066-68, 1117-19; Wayne A. Grudem, *Systematic Theology: An Introduction to Biblical Doctrine* (Leicester, England : Grand Rapids: Inter-Varsity Press; Zondervan Pub. House, 1994), 1100.

16. Francis X. Gumerlock, "The Rapture In An Eleventh-Century Text," *Bibliotheca Sacra* 176, no. 701 (2019), 81.

17. See footnote 3.

18. Dave MacPherson, *The Incredible Cover-up: The True Story on the Pre-Trib Rapture*, rev. and combined ed. (Plainfield, NJ: Logos International, 1975), xi.

19. Hitchcock, *Could the Rapture Happen Today?*, 17.

20. Ibid., 17-19.

21. *The MacArthur Study Bible*, gen. ed., John MacArthur (Nashville: Word Publishing, 1997), 1860, n. 1:2.

22. Spiros Zodhiates, *The Complete Word Study Dictionary: New Testament*, electronic ed. (Chattanooga, TN: AMG Publishers, 2000), s.v., ἐλπίζω, elpízō.

23. Charles C. Ryrie, *Everyman's Bible Commentary: First & Second Thessalonians* (Chicago: Moody Press, 1959, 1987, 2001), 60.

24. Zodhiates, *The Complete Word Study Dictionary: New Testament*, s.v., παρακαλέω, parakaléō.

25. Ibid., s.v., Φθάνω, phthánō.

26. Compare Matthew 24:31

27. Jerry Sutton, *The Baptist Reformation: The Conservative*

Resurgence in the Southern Baptist Convention (Nashville: Broadman & Holman, 2000), 33.

28. I marvel that you are turning away so soon from Him who called you in the grace of Christ, to a different gospel, which is not another; but there are some who trouble you and want to pervert the gospel of Christ. But even if we, or an angel from heaven, preach any other gospel to you than what we have preached to you, let him be accursed. As we have said before, so now I say again, if anyone preaches any other gospel to you than what you have received, let him be accursed. For do I now persuade men, or God? Or do I seek to please men? For if I still pleased men, I would not be a bondservant of Christ (Gal 1:6-10).

29. See, Mark H. Ballard and Timothy K. Christian, *Words Matter: What Is the Gospel?* (Bennington, VT: Northeastern Baptist Press, 2020); Ronnie W. Rogers, *A Corruption of Consequence: Adding Social Justice to the Gospel*, 2021; Mark H. Ballard and Timothy K. Christian, eds., *Does it Still Matter?: Essays in Honor of the Conservative Resurgence* (Bennington, VT: Northeastern Baptist Press Academic, 2022), note in particular, the "Introduction"; Chapter 1: "Does Inerrancy Still Matter?"; Chapter 2: "Does the Gospel Still Matter?"; Chapter 11: "Does the Conservative Resurgence Still Matter?".

30. David L. Allen and Steve W. Lemke, *The Return of Christ: A Premillennial Perspective*, 2011, accessed September 6, 2021, http://www.vlebooks.com/vleweb/product/openreader?id=none&isbn=9781433675812.

31. See for example: Psalm 22 and Isaiah 52:13-53:12.

32. See 1 Thessalonians 4:16; Ephesians 1:7, 12-14

33. Frederick William Danker, *A Greek-English Lexicon of the New Testament and other Early Christian Literature*, BDAG, 3rd ed. (Chicago: The University of Chicago Press, 1957, 1979, 2000), s.v. "φθαρτὸν".

34. Danker, BDAG, s.v. "ἀφθαρσίαν".

35. D. K. Lowery, "1 Corinthians" in, *The Bible Knowledge*

Commentary: An Exposition of the Scriptures, vol. 2, eds., John F. Walvoord and Roy B. Zuck (Wheaton, IL: Victor Books, 1985), 546.

36. Grudem, *Systematic Theology*, 864.

37. This is now a very common statement in Baptist life. My first memory of hearing the statement came from Daniel Akin, who taught it in numerous classes at the Criswell College in Dallas, TX in the 1980s. However, I believe the idea of an "inaugurated eschatology" originated with Oscar Cullman, who modified C. H. Dodd's "realized eschatology" to include a 'now, but not yet' understanding of the Kingdom. George Eldon Ladd popularized the concept in the United States. Ladd's work influenced progressive dispensationalists.

38. Ronnie Floyd, Chapel Sermon at Northeastern Baptist College. Bennington, VT, September 15, 2015.

39. Hitchcock, *Can We Still Believe in the Rapture?*, Kindle Location 1037.

40. Isaiah 2:4; Micah 4:3

41. Paige Patterson, *The Troubled Triumphant Church: An Exposition of First Corinthians* (Fort Worth, Tex.: Seminary Hill Press, 2011), 304.

42. Romans 6:10; Hebrews 7:27; 9:12; 10:10

43. Acts 17:1–10

44. Acts 17:2–3

45. 1 Thessalonians 4:13–18

46. 1 Thessalonians 5:1–11

47. Acts 17:9–10

48. J. P. Lange, P. Schaff, C. A. Auberlen, C. J. Riggenbach, and J. Lillie, *A Commentary on the Holy Scriptures: 1 & 2 Thessalonians* (Bellingham, WA: Logos Bible Software, 2008), 72.

49. R. Jamieson, A. R. Fausset, and D. Brown, *Commentary Critical and Explanatory on the Whole Bible*, vol. 2 (Oak Harbor, WA: Logos Research Systems, Inc., 1997), 389–90.

50. Ken Larson, *I & II Thessalonians, I & II Timothy, Titus, Philemon*, vol. 9 (Nashville, TN: Broadman & Holman Publishers, 2000), 57.

51. 1 Thessalonians 4:18

52. Norman L. Geisler, *Systematic Theology: in one vol.* (Minneapolis, MN: Bethany House Publishers, 2011), 1213.

53. Reading this paragraph may raise the question of an additional theological debate. Some theologians believe humans are made up of body and soul, while others believe humans are composed of body, soul, and spirit. While those who argue for "soul sleep" have clearly fallen into biblical and theological error, both dichotomists and trichotomists, who carefully apply a consistent grammatical-historical hermeneutic, avoid this error. The debate over whether man is a dichotomy, or a trichotomy is beyond the scope of this book. Suffice it to say, for both biblical and theological reasons, the present authors believe humans to have a body, soul, and a spirit.

54. Charles C. Ryrie, *Everyman's Bible Commentary: First & Second Thessalonians.*

55. "He will swallow up death forever, and the Lord God will wipe away tears from all faces; the rebuke of His people He will take away from all the earth; for the Lord has spoken" (Isa 25:8); "I will ransom them from the power of the grave; I will redeem them from death. O Death, I will be your plagues! O Grave, I will be your destruction! Pity is hidden from My eyes" (Hos 13:14).

56. Charles Hodge, *An Exposition of the First Epistle to the Corinthians* (Grand Rapids: Baker Book House, 1857, 1980), 357-78.

57. The only known exceptions to the rule are Enoch (Gen 5:24; Heb 11:5) and Elijah (2 Kgs 2:11).

58. Zodhiates, *The Complete Word Study Dictionary: New Testament*, s.v., κέντρον, kéntron.

59. R. J. Utley, *Paul's Letters to a Troubled Church: 1 and 2 Corinthians*, vol. 6, (Marshall, TX: Bible Lessons International, 2002), 6:184.

60. "Synoptic" means to see together.

61. Here is the reason the 4 gospels do not record most of His miracles: "And there are also many other things that Jesus did, which if they were written one by one, I suppose that even the world itself could not contain the books that would be written. Amen" (John 21:25). The miracles recorded in the gospels are but a tiny fraction of the multitude of miracles Jesus the Messiah performed. The ones recorded are not the whole, but representatives of the whole. Our Bible is inspired by God (2 Tim 3:16), and contains everything we need to know for life and Godliness. Nothing included or excluded is accidental. On a practical level, we can be thankful. The Bible is an ideal, manageable size. God planned it that way. Remember that next time you pick up your Bible. If everything Jesus did and said were recorded, a freight train couldn't haul it; and forget about your pocket-sized New Testament or a checkbook-sized Bible in your purse.

62. Matthew 26:26-29; Mark 14:22-25; Luke 22:19-20

63. Daniel A. Carson, *The Gospel According to John* (Grand Rapids: William B. Eerdmans Publishing Co., 1991), 476, 510.

64. Hitchcock, *Can We Still Believe in the Rapture?*; Shekinah Of Glory Ministries Blogger, "Scripture in Light of '1st Century History': Jewish Wedding Customs," *Scripture in Light of "1st Century History,"* May 15, 2011, accessed September 10, 2021, http://newjerusalemcommunity.blogspot.com/2011/05/jewish-wedding-customs.html; "Ancient Jewish Wedding Customs and Yeshua's Second Coming," *Messianic Bible*, n.d., accessed September 10, 2021, https://free.messianicbible.com/feature/ancient-jewish-wedding-customs-and-yeshuas-second-coming/; "(1) (DOC) Three Foundational Rapture Passages | Robert Dean,

Jr. – Academia.Edu," accessed September 11, 2021, https://www.academia.edu/42024447/Three_Foundational_Rapture_Passages.

65. Matthew 19:1-10. See also Joseph's consideration in Matthew 1:18-25.

66. A good docudrama that will help you become familiar with 'First Century Jewish Wedding' customs is: "Before the Wrath," *Pure Flix*, accessed September 10, 2021, https://app.pureflix.com/videos/391012390456/before-the-wrath. Commentary provided by several scholars including: Jay McCarl, a Middle East Anthropologist; Jan Markell of Olive Tree Ministries; J.D. Farag, a Theologian and Senior Pastor; Jack Hibbs, Theologian and Senior Pastor; Amir Tsarfati of Behold Israel; Scott McConnell of LifeWay Research; and Lizette Dillinger the Qualitative Director at LifeWay Research.

67. Revelation 19:6-8

68. Not all commentators believe this passage refers to the Lord's return. Borchert notes Dodd and others who suggest this is about Jesus coming to receive a follower at the time of his/her death. However, he concludes his discussion, acknowledging the likelihood that it indeed has an eschatological view in mind. Gerald L. Borchert, John 12-21, in *The New American Commentary*, vol. 25B (Nashville: Broadman & Holman, 2002), 105-106. Merrill Tenney argues that this text cannot be referring to death, but must be focused on the eschatological return of Jesus. Frank Ely Gaebelein, ed., *John - Acts, in The Expositor's Bible Commentary*, vol. 9 (London: Pickering & Inglis, 1981), 143. Walvoord agrees that this text has an eschatological return of Jesus in mind and in no way speaks to Jesus coming at one's personal death. John F. Walvoord, *The Rapture Question* (Findlay, OH: Dunham Publishing Company, 1957), 75-76.

69. cf., Matthew 24

70. For a helpful discussion of the contrast between Matthew 24 and John 14:3, see John F. Walvoord, *The Rapture Question*, 108-111.

71. Ephesians 5:24–32

72. Genesis 3:6

73. J. Dwight Pentecost, "Daniel" in *The Bible Knowledge Commentary: An Exposition of the Scriptures,* vol. 1, John F. Walvoord and Roy B. Zuck, eds. (Wheaton: Victor Books, 1985), 1364.

74. Revelation 4–19

75. Hitchcock, *Can We Still Believe in the Rapture?*, Kindle Location 1726.

76. Ibid., 1726–1777.

77. Allen and Lemke, eds., *The Return of Christ A Premillennial Perspective*, Kindle Location 1392–1414.

78. See Matthew 24:5–8

79. Craig L. Blomberg, Matthew in *The New American Commentary*, vol. 22, David S. Dockery, gen. ed. (Nashville: Broadman & Holman Publishers, 1992), 354.

80. The preterist view believes that John was speaking of things relating to his own day and the days in the near future to John's writing. This view holds that most of the book is about events taking place in the first century. For more on this see Paige Patterson, Revelation, in The New American Commentary, vol. 39, gen. ed., David S. Dockery (Nashville: B&H Publishing, 2012), 27.

81. "Belief in the Rapture," *Lifeway Research*, accessed September 11, 2021; https://lifewayresearch.com/search/Belief in the Rapture/.

82. Allen and Lemke, *The Return of Christ A Premillennial Perspective*, Kindle Location 1332–1343.

83. "Belief in the Rapture," *Lifeway Research*, accessed September 11, 2021; https://lifewayresearch.com/search/Belief in the Rapture/.

84. Gleason L. Archer, ed., *Three Views on the Rapture: Pre-, Mid-, or Post-Tribulation*, Counterpoints (Grand Rapids, MI: Zondervan, 1996).

85. Archer, *Three Views on the Rapture*, 211.

86. Ibid., 171.

87. Ibid., 171–211.

88. Ibid., 223–231.

89. "Belief in the Rapture," *Lifeway Research*, accessed September 11, 2021; https://lifewayresearch.com/search/Belief in the Rapture/.

90. Johnny V. Boley, *Another Look at the Rapture* (Unpublished, n.d.).

91. Boley argues that the first three and a half years of Daniel's 70th week should be understood as having taken place during Jesus' public ministry on earth. He believed Jesus' crucifixion and resurrection halted God's prophetic timeline, as God deals with the world through the Church rather than through the nation of Israel. He believed at some point in the future, just prior to the revelation of the Antichrist, the Rapture will take place and the second half of Daniel's 70th week will begin. Thus, he refers to his view as "pre-tribulation but mid-week."

92. Archer, *Three Views on the Rapture*, 115.

93. Ibid.

94. Marvin J. Rosenthal, *The Pre-Wrath Rapture of the Church* (Nashville: T. Nelson, 1990).

95. Renald E. Showers, *The Pre-Wrath Rapture View: An Examination and Critique* (Grand Rapids: Kregel Publications, 2001).

96. "Belief in the Rapture," *Lifeway Research*, accessed September 11, 2021; https://lifewayresearch.com/search/Belief in the Rapture/.

97. Showers, *The Pre-Wrath Rapture View*, 10–11.

98. Renald Showers, *Maranatha Our Lord, Come! A Definitive Study of the Rapture of the Church* (Bellmawr, NJ: The Friends of Israel Gospel Ministry, Inc., 1995), 13.

99. Showers, *Maranatha Our Lord, Come!*, 170.

100. Walvoord, *The Rapture Question*, 105.

101. Ira E. David, "Translation: When Does It Occur?" *The Dawn*, November 15, 1935, 358; quoted in Walvoord, The Rapture Question, 105.

102. Walvoord, *The Rapture Question*, 108.

103. Walvoord, *The Rapture Question*, 106–108.

104. I use the word "us" intentionally. I am included among the saints of all the ages. This is not arrogance or pride. It is a praise statement. It humbles me. Saints are neither perfect nor super-spiritual. Saints are sinners who were convicted of personal sins, realized Jesus Christ was punished on the cross for all those sins, and trusted Him alone for their salvation. Saints are saved by grace through faith in Jesus Christ, and I am in that throng. Are you?

I believed the Gospel and received Jesus when I was 7 years old. He has never left me and will never leave me nor forsake me. That's Jesus' promise (Heb 13:5-6). You too will be in that number if you have received Jesus Christ by faith. If you are unsure of how to be saved, please turn to the Appendix at the end of this book: "HOW TO BE SURE YOU WON'T BE LEFT BEHIND." It is urgent!

105. Patterson, *NAC: Revelation*, 171. This statement is based on the understanding that the 24 elders in some fashion represent the church, raptured and worshiping around the throne. As Patterson notes, "How then, … are the 24 elders to be interpreted? The answer is that the 12 sons of Jacob represent the 12 tribes of Israel, and the 12 apostles of the Lamb represent the church. This conclusion is perfectly consistent with … [Jesus' promise to] the disciples in Matt 19:28, … 'I tell you the truth, at the renewal of all things, when the Son of Man sits on his glorious throne, you who have followed me will also sit on twelve thrones, judging the twelve tribes of Israel.'"

106. C. I. Scofield and Henry G. Weston, *The Holy Bible Containing the Old and New Testaments: Authorized King James Version with a New System of Connected Topical References*

to All the Greater Themes of Scripture, with Annotations, Revised Marginal Renderings, Summaries, Definitions, Chronology, and Index, to Which Are Added, Helps at Hard Places, Explanations of Seeming Discrepancies, and a New System of Paragraphs, 1945.

107. Pastor of First Baptist Church, Dallas, Texas

108. Pastor of Bellevue Baptist Church, Memphis, Tennessee

109. President of Criswell College, Dallas, TX; Southeastern Baptist Theological Seminary, Wake Forest, NC; Southwestern Baptist Theological Seminary, Fort Worth, TX

110. Billy Graham, *Approaching Hoofbeats: The Four Horsemen of the Apocalypse* (Waco, TX: Word Books, 1984).

111. Donald W. Thompson et al., *A Thief in the Night*, Drama, Fantasy, Horror (Mark IV Pictures Incorporated, 1973).

112. Donald W. Thompson et al., *A Distant Thunder*, Drama, Sci-Fi (Mark IV Pictures Incorporated, 1978).

113. Donald W. Thompson et al., *Image of the Beast*, Sci-Fi, Thriller (Mark IV Pictures Incorporated, 1981).

114. "The Alternative Jesus: Psychedelic Christ," TIME; https://content.time.com/time/subscriber/article/0,33009,905202-3,00.html, accessed 28 September 2022.

115. If you wish to hear the song, access it at: Larry Norman - *I Wish We'd All Been Ready* - [1989], 2013; accessed September 15, 2021, https://www.youtube.com/watch?v=aPJpZdEOILQ.

116. Edgar C. Whisenant, *88 Reasons Why the Rapture Is in 1988* (Edgar C. Whisenant, 1988).

117. Christopher Hutton, "The Legacy Of Harold Camping, Who Falsely Predicted The World's End, Lives On"; https://religionunplugged.com/news/2021/5/21/the-legacy-of-harold-camping-who-falsely-predicted-the-worlds-end-lives-on, (accessed 3 Oct 2022).

118. Tim LaHaye and Jerry B. Jenkins, *The Left Behind Collection* (Wheaton: Tyndale House Publishers, 2014).

119. Tim LaHaye, *No Fear of the Storm* (Sisters, OR: Multnomah, 1992); Tim LaHaye and Jerry B Jenkins, *Are We Living in the End Times?* (Wheaton: Tyndale House Publishers, 2001); Tim LaHaye, *The Merciful God of Prophecy: His Loving Plan for You in the End Times* (New York: Warner Books, 2002).

120. Hitchcock, *Can We Still Believe in the Rapture?*, Kindle Location 425-433.

121. "Belief in the Rapture," *Lifeway Research*, accessed September 11, 2021; https://lifewayresearch.com/search/Belief in the Rapture/.

122. Charles C. Ryrie, *Dispensationalism*, rev. and updated (Chicago: Moody Press, 1995), 81.

123. The 69 weeks of years, 7 x 69 = 483 years, began with Artaxerxes Longimanus's decree (445 BC) to rebuild Jerusalem (Neh 2:1-9) and ended with the Passover when Jesus made His Triumphal Entry, was crucified, and resurrected. For an extended discussion of the prophecy's literal fulfillment see: LaHaye and Hindson, Exploring Bible Prophecy, 243-58.

124. See, Tim LaHaye, *Understanding Bible Prophecy for Yourself* (Eugene, OR: Harvest House Publishers, 1998, 2001), 92.

125. Ibid., 53.

ABOUT THE AUTHORS

Dr. Mark H. Ballard serves as the Publisher for Northeastern Baptist Press, and President of Northeastern Baptist College in Bennington, VT. He has served as a faithful pastor, diligent church planter, passionate evangelist, innovative educator, creative and prolific author, pacesetting Baptist leader, and is the husband of Cindy and dad of Benjamin. He graduated Criswell College with his Bachelor's, and Southeastern Baptist Theological Seminary with his M.Div. and Ph.D. Dr. Ballard has filled pulpits, held revival services, and served as a conference speaker in numerous states for more than 40 years.

Timothy K. Christian is a retired pastor and professor, now living in Martinsville, VA. He pastored churches in the southeast, northeast, and in Naples, Italy. Dr. Christian served as a professor and administrator at Mid-America Baptist Theological Seminary and a professor at Northeastern Baptist College. Tim has been married to his friend Judy since 1976. They have two married children, and seven grandchildren. In retirement Tim writes part-time and is the full-time caregiver for Judy as she battles advanced Secondary Progressive MS.